What Makes People

T I C K

How to Understand Yourself and Others

Des Hunt

First publication 1988 by Intell Publishing Pty. Ltd.

Second publication 1991 by McGraw-Hill Book Company Pty. Ltd.

Third publication 1997 by Personal & Professional Growth Concepts Pty. Ltd.

Reprinted 2003 by Personal & Professional Growth Concepts Pty. Ltd.

Reprinted 2005 by Personal & Professional Growth Concepts Pty. Ltd.

Reprinted 2014 2nd Revised Edition by AWC Business Solutions Pty. Ltd.

A CiP number can be found at the National Library of Australia

Available in print and as an ebook.

ISBN: 978-0-9925553-4-4 (pbk) 2nd Revised Edition
ISBN: 978-0-9925553-5-1 (ebk)

Published by: AWC Business Solutions Pty Ltd
PO Box 282, Kensington Park, South Australia 5068
Phone (08) 8463 1986
Email: info@tick.com.au
Website: www.tick.com.au

**This book is dedicated to the
three women in my life**

Val, Tracy and Julie

BOOKS BY DES HUNT

What Makes People Tick

How to Sell the Way Your Customer Buys

I Love You But How Do I Live With You?

SPEAKING AND SEMINARS

Des Hunt is an international speaker and seminar leader based
in Adelaide, Australia. For information about his speaking
presentations and seminars based on the 'What Makes People
Tick' concepts, please contact the address below.

AWC Business Solutions Pty Ltd
PO Box 282 Kensington Park, South Australia 5068
Phone: Australia (08) 8463 1986
email: info@tick.com.au
Website: www.tick.com.au

NOTICE TO TRAINERS AND HUMAN RESOURCE PROFESSIONALS

It is a breach of copyright and illegal to use any of the materials contained in this book including the bird symbols to depict personality styles.

Des Hunt's range of powerful training and human resource development materials and tools using the 'What Makes People Tick' principles and copyrighted bird symbols, are available for use under license to Human Resource professionals.

Part of these materials include the 'Personal Insight Profile Indicator Questionnaire' which is a far more comprehensive and accurate questionnaire than the one in this book, and is accompanied by the '16 Mini-Profiles Report' which are sold together as a pack.

Other materials available using the 'What Makes People Tick' principles and copyrighted bird graphics include notes on: Communicating, Team Building, Leading, Managing, Selling, Relationship Strategies and more. See following page.

For details on how to become a licensed user of the 'What Makes People Tick' materials contact:

AWC Business Solutions Pty Ltd
PO Box 282 Kensington Park, SA 5068
Phone (08) 8463 1968
Email: info@tick.com.au
Website: www.tick.com.au

What Makes People
T I C K

How to Understand
Yourself and Others

Des Hunt

CONTENTS

Section Three: Questionnaire and Profiles 63

Section Four: Square Pegs in Square Holes 109

INTRODUCTION

This book is about understanding human nature.

It is about being able to identify and understand the basic personality styles - their strengths, their weaknesses, their natural inclinations, perceptions, skills and capabilities.

It is about looking further than our impressions and natural inclinations perceived from our own comfortable but distorted windows of reality, and it's about attempting to see the reality of others - to see their view of life - and to understand it. At the least, this understanding can provide us with the power of empathy: the ability to walk in another's shoes. Empathy in action is also what this book is about.

When used in our personal lives, applying these principles can lead to fuller relationships, better communication and, above all, understanding what makes us different and appreciating that difference. When used in managing others, they can lead to stronger working relationships, better use of individual talents, stronger team spirit, and ultimately increased productivity.

When used in our business lives, these principles can increase our effectiveness in communicating, negotiating and dealing with people - which is the real business of business. The people business.

Observing human nature and trying to understand it, has been the subject of many thinkers throughout history. As far back as AD 160 the Greek physician and philosopher, Galen, was writing about the four basic 'temperaments' of human nature, how the characteristics could be observed, and how certain behaviour could be predicted according to which temperament one possessed.

Over 1700 years later, around 1920, the psychologist Carl Jung was writing about 'types', explaining how behaviour had certain observable patterns based on four basic mental functions, and again, like Galen, pointing out how certain behaviour is predictable within types.

I have taken a blend of Galen, Jung and others and added my own thoughts and experiences. To this mix I have also added a pinch of creative imagination so that it is presented in a way which I hope is both enjoyable to read and easy to understand.

This is not intended to be a theoretical treatise. Rather, it is written in plain simple language so that it will be understood and used - because understanding is what this book is all about. It is by necessity a traveler's guide - a broad road map which offers directions - which I hope will be useful because of its simplicity.

We all have strengths, and we all have acceptable weaknesses. By being able to identify those strengths, as well as understanding the acceptable weaknesses, we can tap into and use the potential of those around us. This is the basic principle of people management.

Like sports and hobbies, we all have our natural aptitudes, skills and talents. We are all 'naturals' at something. One of the secrets of all successful coaches, leaders and managers is that they 'play' their people in the positions where they can best display and use their natural abilities. They allow their people to 'shine'. Knowing where they shine is half the secret.

It pains me to see so much creativity, productivity and ultimately profitability lost, simply through not being able to identify, and then utilise, the natural skills and abilities of different styles of people. Being able to identify those styles is also what this book is about.

The cost of putting square pegs in round holes in terms of de-motivation, stress, unhappiness and decreased productivity is incalculable. This book will help avoid this mistake.

Making people fit jobs ignores any consideration of natural skills and talents and defies the laws of human nature which tell us that we always enjoy what we are good at doing, and that we are always motivated by the things which interest us. The quickest way to de-motivate someone is to threaten his or her self-interest. It is all a matter of 'different strokes for different folks'. Helping to provide those strokes, and when, is also what this book is about.

'Eagles' are decisive, result-oriented, and seek a free rein and if they don't get it, they become frustrated. Given the same freedom the 'Owl' may become lost for want of an adequate structure. When promoting an idea or innovation the 'Peacock' is in its element. Given the same task the 'Dove' is in foreign territory. Asking a 'Peacock' or an 'Eagle' to be a supportive and compliant member of a team is to misjudge their natural inclinations. Expecting a quick reaction to change from an 'Owl' or a 'Dove' is to ignore their natural tendencies.

Giving a job to an 'Owl' that a 'Peacock' should be doing, or giving a task to an 'Eagle' that a 'Dove' is better equipped to do, not only wastes the natural resources of our human assets but also causes them untold stress, ulcers and heart attacks. How to avoid those stresses is included in this book.

It has been said that the difference between love and hate lies in understanding. That is to say, when we understand *why* somebody does something that irks us, it is difficult to dislike him or her for it. This book will help in gaining a better understanding of the 'Why'.

It has also been said that we waste a lot of energy arguing for agreement rather than striving for understanding. Understanding each other is far more important than agreement. This book strives for that understanding. It is about appreciating human nature. For better or for worse.

It seems to me that the comparatively short time we spend on this planet is taken up with a lot of misunderstanding which takes much of the enjoyment out of life. Anything that can help alleviate some of that misunderstanding has to be worth talking about. That is really the bottom line of this book - enjoying life.

SECTION ONE

OUR
WINDOWS
OF LIFE

HOW COME THEY CAN DO IT?

It has always fascinated me that some people are naturals at some things and other people aren't. It intrigued me that some people could make things I find difficult to do look like child's play.

For years I castigated myself about the things I wasn't good at while overlooking and taking for granted all the things I was good at. Perhaps that is all part of being human. Other people tell me they do the same thing. For years I looked at those I admired, seeing only the qualities and talents I seemed to lack, little knowing then that all of us have our own characteristic strengths - and our corresponding weaknesses.

Human nature, like most things in life, is a two-way street. We all have our strengths and we all have our weaknesses. And to a large extent, given our nature, these are quite predictable and acceptable. We are all good at some things, and we are all not so good at other things.

PERSONAL GROWTH   Knowing and admiring our own strengths and recognising and accepting our weaknesses, and then working on them is, I believe, the first step to personal growth and the first major step to gaining self-esteem and confidence. This, in turn, helps us to achieve the things we feel are important to us in life.

WHY CAN'T YOU SEE IT MY WAY?

Have you noticed how some people have an almost set and predictable pattern to the way they think, act and speak? Some people are so predictable that 'we know what they're thinking before they think it'.

HABITS OF BEHAVIOUR People have habits of behaviour. They are generally consistent in the way they think, act and react in a given situation.

Shy people react to groups of strangers in the same way, while others appear confident and outgoing no matter what the company. Some people are always concerned about the welfare of those around them, while others seem to walk through life as if other people and their feelings hardly exist. And they all seem to do this as if they were programmed by some predetermined pattern.

Have you ever noticed how some people's opinions seem to be based on entirely different information to what you have; yet you all heard the same information? It's as though they are wired with a completely different circuit from yours!

A TOTALLY DIFFERENT WINDOW Have you also noticed that some people have a completely different outlook on life from yours? That they place importance on things that you feel to be quite trivial? That they seem to look at life, and the things that are happening around them, from an entirely different point of view to you? They seem to be looking out of a totally different window of life from yours and seeing a totally different view. Well, they are.

OUR WAVES OF DISTORTION

All glass, no matter how 'perfect' it appears, has in-built waves of distortion.

Our view of reality through our 'glass' (that is, the way we look at life and other people) is distorted as we look through these waves. But where do these waves come from? Who put them in our glass? Are we born with them or are they conditioned into us?

Psychologists and biologists have been talking about those questions for ages. In fact, they even have a name for it: 'The nature or nurture debate'. I believe it is influenced by both our genes and by our upbringing - those things and people that were influencing us as we grew up.

By the time we reach our teens our perceptions have been clouded or distorted by the values, opinions, judgments and expectations of those around us. Eventually reality, that is *our own view of reality*, is what we see through these conditioned waves of distortion.

Reality is how we see it. What we see is what
we believe and what we believe is what we see.

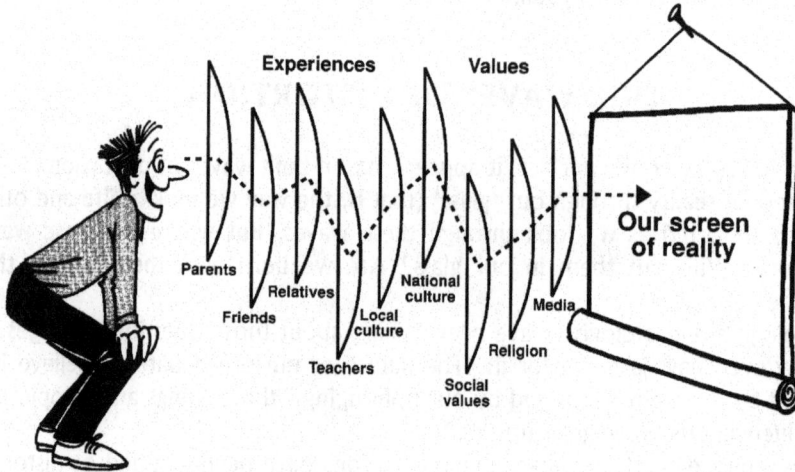

Looking Through Our Lenses of Distortion

OUR WINDOWS OF LIFE

We all have our own way of viewing life and the way we seem to fit into it. It's as if we each have a 'room with a view' with our own special window. And through this window we see and interpret life and other people. The view we have depends on where our room and window is placed in our 'building of life'.

Not only are our personal windows in different positions, but the glass within each window has different 'waves of distortion'. It is through this distortion that we see what we believe to be reality.

IT MAKES US WHO WE ARE Whether our reality is fact makes no difference to us. Reality as we see it and believe it, makes up the fabric of our lives. It makes us who we are.

By knowing the window another person looks out of, by 'seeing' their view of life and how they fit into it, can give us the key to understanding what makes other people tick. It can also offer us the opportunity for a true sense of empathy;

the ability to walk in another's shoes, to see and feel life as it appears through their window.

THE BUSINESS OF LIFE Understanding how other people see life can help us appreciate the differences between us, and give us an insight into how to adapt to those differences. It can be the key to better interpersonal relationships, better working relationships, better teamwork, and to a better understanding of the business of life; the people business.

Understanding the windows of life shows us that the golden rule of 'Do unto others as you would have them do unto you' would be better amended to 'Do unto others as they would wish it done unto them'. In other words, your way may not be their way.

OTHER PEOPLE'S WINDOWS An understanding of where other people's windows are situated proves that there are 'Different strokes for different folks'. Understanding can help us to know what strokes to use for what folks.

It can also help us to understand ourselves better. To understand self is one of the greatest understandings one can possess. It can show us why we seem to be strong in some areas yet so weak in others. It can help us continue to develop and capitalise on our strengths and pinpoint the areas where we are not so strong. Then we can work on them or accept them for what they are - those things which make us human. Those things which make us who we are.

Understanding how other people see life is
the key to understanding the people business.

THE FOUR BASIC WINDOWS

We could be excused for thinking that there should be thousands of windows to
suit the thousands of different outlooks in life. Yet people who have spent a
lifetime studying and observing human nature tend to agree that a person's view of
life is made up of a combination of just four basic windows, styles, or human
characteristics.

A PREFERRED VIEW It would, of course, be nonsense to suggest that we all fit
neatly into only one of four basic windows. Human nature is far too complex for
that. The truth is that we possess differing degrees of views from each window. But
we do have preferred or dominant windows that influence or bias our view and
generally there are two windows. In other words, experience shows that most
people have a dominant window and a secondary, less dominant, window through
which they perceive life and reality.

MOTIVATING FORCES If you know people's preferred windows you will
know what motivates and drives them, what urges them on, where their strengths
lie, what areas of natural skills they possess, their likes and dislikes in certain
situations, the things they feel comfortable doing, and the things they are not so
good at. And what demotivates them.

OUR COMFORT ZONES Obviously in our day-to-day lives when we have to
deal with different situations and the demands of others, there are many times
when we have to 'step out of character' and leave our comfort zone, move from
our window, fit in with the needs of others or work to somebody else's view of
how things should be done. In other words, 'fit in'.

However, being human, after conforming or working to another's point of
view, we will always wish to return to our own window. That is where we are in
control. That is where we feel comfortable. That is where 'I' can be naturally 'I',
away from the pressures of the world and those who want to push us from our
comfort zones. We always return to the windows that give us the view we want to
see.

THE BUILDING OF LIFE

Imagine that all the people in the world live in a two-storey building with four rooms, two on the ground floor and two on the top floor. Imagine also that all the people who live on the right-hand side of the building tend to be rather shy and a little withdrawn, preferring to listen rather than do most of the talking. The people who live on the left-hand side of the building tend to be confident and assertive and quicker paced than their neighbours on the right. They prefer to talk rather than listen.

DOWNSTAIRS IS COOL   Now imagine that all the people who live on the ground floor are a little on the cool side. They tend to be rather stiff and formal with strangers. These people, if given the chance, would rather get things done alone than have to deal with other people. *They are the Thinkers and Doers.*

UPSTAIRS IS WARM   Finally, imagine that the people who live on the top floor tend to be warmer and friendlier than their neighbours down below. The people on the top floor like the company of other people. They would much prefer to do things in the company of others rather than do them alone. *They are the Feelers and Relators.*

Remember that we are only talking about the four basic extremes at this stage.

Warms

Confidents   **Shys**

Cools

THE BUILDING OF LIFE

Warm and friendly
Prefers to deal with people than do tasks
Feelers: Heart over head

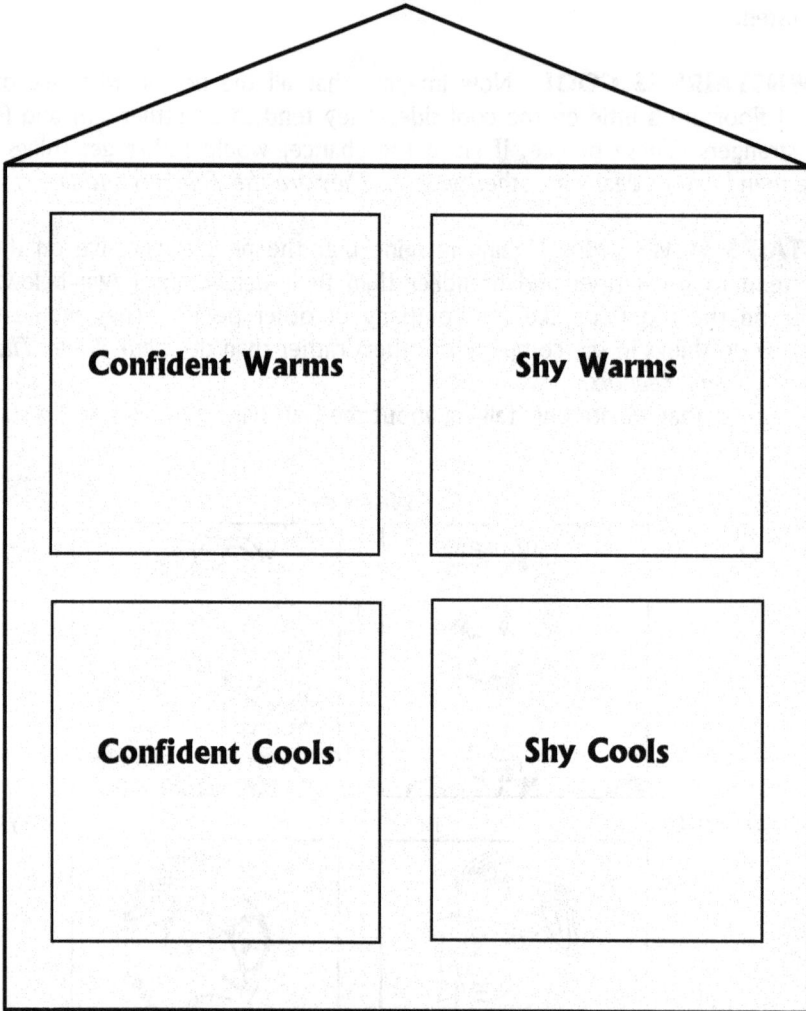

Confident Warms	Shy Warms
Confident Cools	**Shy Cools**

Cool and aloof
Prefers to do tasks than deal with people
Thinkers: Head over heart

Confident warm

"Let me tell you how I did it. Watch this! Great isn't it? Have you seen my new red car?"

Shy warm

"Let's not upset anyone. People and their feelings are important. Relationships are what life is really all about. Be kind."

Confident cool

"Look, I just haven't got the time for all this. I haven't got all day. Get on with it. Forget the questions, just do as I say. Next!"

Shy cool

"I really haven't got enough information yet, or worked out a system. Let me think about it and I'll get back to you. You can't rush these things."

BIRDS OF A FEATHER

To help with descriptions, I have borrowed names from the bird world to describe the people who live in the different rooms. I have found in my seminars that most people enjoy this approach. It's fun and it helps to avoid using sterile labels.

Warm and friendly
Prefer people over tasks
Feelers: Heart over head

Confident warm

THE PEACOCK

Warm shy

THE DOVE

Confident cool

THE EAGLE

Shy Cool

THE OWL

Cool and aloof
Prefer tasks over people
Thinkers: Head over heart

Remember that most people view life from more than one window. But more on that later. For now, let's look at the descriptions of the four basic styles: the Peacock, the Eagle, the Dove and the Owl.

The Peacock is a colourful, showy bird. It struts around proudly and likes to be admired. If you don't happen to notice it, it will get your attention by fanning its tail feathers for all to see. You can't ignore the Peacock, it will let you know it's there, one way or another. It likes to be the centre of attention.

The Dove is a peaceful, modest and sensitive bird. It is gentle, quiet and unobtrusive. It cares about the other birds and suffers quietly if any harm is done to it. It likes to be a caring and supportive part of the flock.

The Eagle soars high. It controls its domain and all other birds within it. It generally gets what it sets its sights on and flies in a direct, unwavering line towards its objective. It perches high up in the cliffs away from the other birds. It likes to be the boss.

The Owl is a quiet, intense bird. It is unobtrusive, preferring to do its thinking, which it does a lot of, away from the company of other birds. It likes its own space and time to think, analyse and ponder. It likes the security of a predictable habitat. It likes to be precise and right.

THE PEACOCK

The Peacock is a colourful and showy bird. It struts its stuff proudly and likes to be noticed and admired. And if you don't happen to notice it, it will get your attention by spreading its tail feathers for all to see. You just can't ignore the Peacock, it will let you know it's there one way or another. It likes to be the centre of attention. To be honest, it's a bit of a showoff.

I AM A PEACOCK

I'm happy to be called a Peacock because the Peacock is a dominant and attractive bird. People admire them just like they admire me!

I am a very social person. I like the company of other people. After all is said and done, people are what life is all about. It's important that people like you - isn't it?

I thrive on popularity, applause and recognition of my skills and talents. When I do something good you can't thank me enough. 'Thankyou' is one of the most important words in the English language in my opinion - besides 'Bravo'!

You'll find me wherever there is a group of people. I'll be the one doing most of the talking. I am great at telling jokes and making people laugh. Modesty is not one of my long suits so therefore I can tell you that wherever I go I'm the life of the party. Let's face it, people enjoy my company! OK, so I like being the centre of attention - what's wrong with that?

Because of my impulsiveness and spontaneity, which I would rather call my creativity, and my ability to verbalise (which Owls tend to call a 'gift of the gab'), you will often find me in selling, advertising, television, acting, entertaining, promoting, in fact just about anywhere there is a spotlight and a chance to display my natural talents.

Achievement is very important to me. And letting the world know you've made it is all part of it. OK, so I like the flashy cars, nice home and the other creature comforts. If you've got it - flaunt it I always say. I've always been like that really. Even as a kid my theme was 'Look Mum -no hands!' I like nice things and I let you know what I paid for them even if you don't ask me. Have you seen my trophies and certificates?

I tend to carry my heart on my sleeve. I let my emotions show. Feelings are what it's all about. I want you to know how I'm feeling even if you don't ask me. I must admit I am a bit of a sook when I'm feeling off-colour. And when I lose my temper I can fly off the handle with lots of noise and drama. But, once it's over, I quickly return to my warm lovable self.

On the downside of my normally warm and friendly personality, I should tell you that listening too long without talking really tires me out. Also I detest doing detail work, especially paperwork. That stuff is best left to the Owls, I always say. I'm more the creative person, an ideas person. I'm a far better starter than I am a finisher. Got anyone you want motivated, or something you want sold? That's more up my alley. By the way, have you heard the one about ...

The Peacocks
"Look at me everybody!"

THE DOVE

The Dove is a peaceful, placid and sensitive bird. It is gentle, quiet and unobtrusive. It cares about the other birds, and suffers quietly if any harm is done to it. It likes to be a caring and supportive part of the flock. To be honest, some people see them as a bit wimpy.

I AM A DOVE

People and their feelings are important to me. I care about them. Particularly my family, my friends and most of the people I work with. Although I must admit I don't like Eagles much, they are too inconsiderate about other people's feelings if you ask me. But generally I just like people, well, most of them anyway.

Harmony among people, especially in a relationship, is also very important to me. I hate any kind of conflict. If there is a hint of any argument in the air, I'm off like a shot!

I know I tend to worry too much about other people's problems and concerns, but that's just the way I am. Funny really, isn't it? I guess I'm just on old softy at heart.

I am very supportive and a good team person. I make a good loyal friend and worker who always has a sympathetic and willing ear.

I don't like change much. My friends say I'm a creature of habit. I stay at the same job for a long time. But it's no good chopping and changing around all the time is it - is it?

Perhaps I am a little shy until you get to know me. I certainly don't throw myself all over people like those Peacocks do. I find them a bit on the pushy side to tell you the truth.

At work you'll find a photo of my family on the desk, indoor plants close by, and bandaids and biscuits in my drawer in case someone may need them.

I am sensitive, patient and modest (did I really say that?) and although I don't necessarily agree, those close to me say that I can be quite stubborn at times.

By the way, how is your mother? She was sick wasn't she?

The Doves
"Let's all be friends."

THE EAGLE

The Eagle soars high. It controls its domain and all the other birds within it. It generally gets what it sets its sights on, and flies in a direct unwavering line towards its objective. It perches high up in the cliffs away from the other birds. It likes to be the boss. To be honest, some people see them as a second cousin to Attila the Hun.

I AM AN EAGLE

I really haven't got time to write this nonsense. Time is important to me. I do things with a sense of urgency. Things that get results. Results are all that count in the long run. I need to be doing and getting on with the job, not sitting here philosophising about people who don't interest me much anyway, unless they can deliver the goods. Results, not theories, that's me.

OK, so people call me a workaholic, that doesn't worry me much, in fact nothing that people say worries me all that much.

Achieving and getting results, and gaining a position of authority in order to get them, is important to me. Sure there are times when I jump in feet first. And sure there are times when I land on people's toes, but that's bad luck. 'If you can't stand the heat, then get out of the kitchen', I always say. I'd rather be respected than popular anyway.

I have been called a 'competitive animal' by some people. But it's no good messing about. If you're going to do something, then do it well. My theme is: 'Winning isn't everything - it's the only thing!'

I haven't got the time or the inclination for diplomacy. I'm a bottom-line person. I say what I think with no frills. If you can't handle it, then that's your problem.

You'll find me in a position of authority, or working towards one, in just about any business or organisation; unions, politics, the police force and the military included.

I don't like to be constrained by rules and regulations, but I think they are important for other people. I don't like a lot of detail either, especially verbal detail. I like people to get straight to the point without wasting my time. And I don't like being asked for explanations of why I'm doing something, or people looking over my shoulder. I like to be given a job and then the freedom and authority to get it done - my way.

I am a self-reliant, self-disciplined risk-taker. 'Nothing ventured, nothing gained', I always say. Above all, I love a challenge and the power and the authority to get the job done.

Next!

The Eagles
"Winning isn't everything – it's the only thing!"

THE OWL

The Owl is a quiet, intense bird. It is unobtrusive, preferring to do its thinking, which is does a lot of, away from the company of other birds. It likes its own space and time, to think, to analyse, and ponder. It likes the security of a predictable habitat. It doesn't like change. To be quite honest, some people see them as quite boring.

I AM AN OWL

Analytical thinking is my long suit. I like a logical and reasoned structure to things. I work on information and facts when making decisions, not emotions. They only get you into trouble.

'Fools rush in where wise men fear to tread', I always say. I question things very carefully before taking any risks. In fact, I avoid anything risky at all costs. You could never say I was impulsive. Although it's true to say that some see this as being indecisive. I don't like the spotlight. I'm not a show-off. I'm certainly not like those showy and flamboyant Peacocks, I find them a bit too pushy and frivolous for my liking. I like people who have their feet planted firmly on the ground.

I admit that some people would see me as shy and cool. I don't throw myself all over people, if that's what you describe as being shy and cool. Showing my feelings is definitely not one of my traits. I deal in facts, figures and set procedures, not feelings.

I also admit I can be critical at times, especially when those around me don't follow the correct procedures. Oh, I know they think I am a perfectionist, crossing 't's' and dotting 'i's', but if a job's worth doing then it's worth doing properly.

The Peacock

"I must have lots of praise and compliments. I need to be recognised."

The Dove

"I must feel needed and part of a group. I need to belong."

The Eagle

"I must be the boss. I need control and authority."

The Owl

"I must have predictability and structure. I need to be right."

The Peacock

"I must have lots of praise and compliments. I need to be recognised."

The Dove

"I must feel needed and part of a group. I need to belong."

The Eagle

"I must be the boss. I need control and authority."

The Owl

"I must have predictability and structure. I need to be right."

KNOWING THE PEACOCK

AT A GLANCE Confident, outgoing, witty, warm and friendly, talks a lot.

DESCRIPTION Likes to be the centre of attention. Wants to be popular. Are quick-paced and spontaneous in actions and decisions, sometimes dramatically so. Finds sustained listening without the chance to talk uncomfortable and tiring. Is generally enthusiastic, excitable and optimistic. Tends to jump from one activity to another. Is a good starter but a poor finisher. Can get others excited and caught up in their dreams and ideas through their naturally strong verbal persuasive skills. Likes to be where the action is. They are ambitious and achievement oriented. They are name-droppers and storytellers. They let you know how important they are, and how many important friends they have.

BODY LANGUAGE Body language is fast and very expressive. Lots of facial expressions and sweeping hand gestures accompany their strong verbal persuasive skills. They use strong glowing language that excites and stimulates. They are always on the move.

DRESS AND ENVIRONMENT They like 'nice things'. Appearances are very important. They are concerned with how others see them. Their dress is normally stylish and fashionable, and can be quite flamboyant. They like dominant colours both on them and around their environment. Because recognition and status symbols are important to them, they will go into debt to 'look good'. Their clothes, jewellery, car, house and office are an expression of themselves and their achievements, both real and imagined. Their work desk normally looks as if a hurricane has just been through their office.

LIFE THEME 'If you've got it, flaunt it.'

MAJOR DRIVING FORCES Ambition and achievement in order to get recognition, applause and popularity for who they are, and what they can do. Being in the spotlight. To be noticed. To be the centre of attention. To be famous.

NATURAL HABITAT Politics, acting, television, evangelism, advertising, marketing, selling, public relations, or anywhere they can be in the spotlight. If they can't find it at work, they will become involved in activities outside of working hours that help satisfy their need for recognition and applause.

STRENGTHS Enthusiastic and optimistic. Ability to motivate others. Good verbal and persuasive skills. Able to think in broad concepts. Ideas generator. Invigorating and animated. Likes people. Able to work quickly and excitingly with others. Risk-takers; will take on new and challenging projects.

SHORTCOMINGS Undisciplined when it comes to time. Dislikes being alone and out of the spotlight. Dislikes detailed analytical work and paperwork in general. Exaggerates and generalises when relating 'facts'. Jumps from one activity to another. Poor finisher. Is excitable, impatient and manipulative when own ends aren't being met. Can be more concerned with people than profit.

UNDER STRESS Under stress Peacocks will fly off the handle with lots of emotion, noise and drama. They will personalise their attacks using strong emotional language. Once over their stress though, they will quickly seek favour and acceptance of the target of their attack. Peacocks fight first and become friendly after. The term 'spitting the dummy' was invented for the Peacock.

TO BE MORE EFFECTIVE To be more effective, the Peacocks need to control their time better, have more sense of urgency. To be less ideological. To have a little more emotional control, and to be firmer with others. They need to slow down a bit so others can keep up with their thoughts and ideas. They can be rather overwhelming and seem to be coming on too strong for some. They should try talking a little less and listening a little more. They could try asking more questions rather than making statements. They would also be more effective getting more facts and figures before rushing into a decision. They need to watch their mood swings. If they are not careful, they can be seen by some as flashy and show-offs.

BOTTOM LINE Peacocks are warm and confident people with special skills which lead them to acting, entertaining, advertising, speaking, people handling, and idea creating roles.

KNOWING THE DOVE

AT A GLANCE Warm, friendly and shy. A sympathetic listener.

DESCRIPTION Supportive, slower paced, warm, people-oriented, shares personal feelings, has a willing ear for problems. A good team member. Reliable and loyal. Pleasant and friendly. Stays in the same job. Avoids risks. Good counselling skills. Good at performing tasks in an accepted work pattern. Sitting or staying in the one place. Doesn't like change. Patient and tolerant. Good at concentrating on, and developing, specialised skills. Placid and peaceful, they make warm loyal friends, co-workers and partners. They like the company of other people and find a sense of security in dealing with people and situations they are familiar with.

BODY LANGUAGE Slower paced and relaxed. Intent listeners. Good eye contact, attentive smiles and nods. Shows interest through facial expressions. Warm, friendly and non-threatening.

DRESS AND ENVIRONMENT Warm pastel colours to bright colours reflect the Dove's natural warmth and supportiveness. Plants, flowers and photographs of their family and friends will be found around them. At work they may well have bandaids, biscuits or sweets in their desk drawer, 'in case somebody should need them'. Their environment is people oriented, warm and welcoming. They prefer to sit on the same side of the desk with you. A poster with the theme of 'caring' may well hang on their office wall. They like to create a 'people-are-important' atmosphere whether at home or at work.

LIFE THEME 'Family, love, and friends are everything.'

MAJOR DRIVING FORCES Security through belonging. To be needed. Dealing with non-threatening people and familiar situations. Same people and places. Habits.

NATURAL HABITAT Supportive roles such as nursing, social work, parenting, counselling, and the other 'helping' professions.

STRENGTHS Warm and supportive. Team worker. Performing tasks in accepted patterns. Concentrating on specialised tasks. Patience, tolerance, loyalty. Good with people.

SHORTCOMINGS   Doves are not good at working in unpredictable environments, nor reacting quickly to change - any change. They are also not good at doing many things at once, or telling people what to do. They shy away from risk situations, irrespective of the opportunities they may present. They are creatures of habit and predictability.

UNDER STRESS When Doves are threatened or under attack they will withdraw, either into themselves or away from the person or situation which is causing stress. Under attack the Dove takes flight and becomes stubborn.

TO BE MORE EFFECTIVE To be more effective, the Dove needs to develop a little more confidence and assertiveness. They need to gain stronger belief in who they are and what they can do. They need to say 'No' more often for their own sake. Speed up a bit and take a few more risks. Spend less time relating to people who don't want - and who perhaps don't deserve - their warmth, loyalty and sincerity.

BOTTOM LINE Doves are warm, shy and timid. Thank goodness there are plenty of them! If the world was full of them, peace would reign forever. Their special skills lead them into teams and people-related helping roles.

KNOWING THE EAGLE

AT A GLANCE Fast, dominant, confident, controlled, cool, abrupt. Doesn't like listening.

DESCRIPTION Fast-paced, confident, assertive and definitely in control of themselves and those around them. Likes to be the boss in any situation. Tells people what to do. Decisive in actions and decisions. Hates inaction and not being in control. Cool, independent and highly competitive. Is impatient with non-performers. Has a very low tolerance for the feelings, attitudes and advice of others. Prefers maximum freedom to manage themselves and others. Can be seen as autocratic, dominant and overbearing when those around them are not living up to their expectations. Will often put work before pleasure. Achievement and results, getting the job done, are everything to the Eagle. They love a challenge. They are the workaholics of life. And they think this book is a load of rubbish!

BODY LANGUAGE Body language is fast and efficient. Expressions are generally cool and controlled. Little emotion shown. Can be abrupt and seemingly uncaring for the little 'people things' happening around them. Often perceived as undiplomatic, critical and bossy. Has little patience with 'small talk'. Will often be heard to say, 'If I want a job done properly, I'm better off doing it myself'.

DRESS AND ENVIRONMENT They are unconcerned with style and fashion. Dress is efficient and practical, as are their surroundings. Generally has planner on wall. Anything that doesn't help in getting results, such as paintings, decor, furnishings and stylish clothing, is considered superfluous. Clothes are normally of sober and conservative colours.

LIFE THEME 'Winning isn't everything - it's the only thing!'

MAJOR DRIVING FORCES Achievement of results through positions of power and authority. Being the boss.

NATURAL HABITAT Politics, police, military, unions, or any business or group which offers the opportunity to attain power and authority.

STRENGTHS   Getting results and causing action. Bringing about change. Accepting a challenge. Making decisions. Getting things done. Solving problems. Taking autocratic leadership roles. Highly self-disciplined.

SHORTCOMINGS   Tends to question authority and work outside the rules, but makes sure others work within them. They are not comfortable being 'just part of the team'. Not good at using caution or calculating the risks. At times can go to uneconomical lengths to achieve goals. Can be disruptive and cause trouble when no challenge or scope is in the job. Low tolerance with 'slower' people. Does not like listening, especially to explanations. Hates excuses. Eagles can be very domineering and insensitive to those around them.

UNDER STRESS   If things aren't going the way Eagles want them to go they will become domineering and bossy, using facts, or logic, or sarcasm, or all three wrapped up in one venomous onslaught. And if things don't get better, the Eagle will turn off, avoid, or ignore either the stressful situation, or the person causing it. When the Eagle loses interest - that's it!

TO BE MORE EFFECTIVE   To be more effective the Eagle needs to take life a little less seriously, to slow down and relax more. They need to acquire more patience and tolerance when dealing with those who are not as fast paced as they are. To not be so rigid and unbending. They need to try dropping back a gear or two and take a little more time to relate to people more. They need to try asking more instead of telling, especially asking other people's opinions, otherwise they run the risk of appearing insensitive, uncaring and impatient. They also need to weigh up the pros and cons a little more before rushing into decisions, particularly in regard to the effect that their quick decisions can have on the people around them, and their feelings.

BOTTOM LINE   Eagles are fast, assertive and a little abrupt, with special skills which lead them to positions of authority. A result in a minimum of time is how they measure their performance.

KNOWING THE OWL

AT A GLANCE Quiet, reserved, shy, cool and distant. Analytical.

DESCRIPTION Thoughtful and introspective. Slower paced and cool. Shows little, if any, feelings or emotions. Hard to get to know. There is a place for everything and everything in its place. Independent, prefers to work alone. Tends to be preoccupied with own thoughts. Cautious and conservative. Not a risk-taker. Always looking for statistics, facts and proof. Suspicious and sceptical. Great respect for rules, procedure, law and order. Only accepts or buys the tried and proven, and the safest. Dislikes social situations. Prefers doing tasks to dealing with people. Is systematic, analytical, persistent, serious and exacting. They often use the saying, 'Fools rush in where wise men fear to tread', as an excuse for indecision and inaction.

BODY LANGUAGE Almost wooden. Little or no animation. Lacks spontaneity. Eye contact is infrequent. Little emotion or facial expression. Poker-faced.

DRESS AND ENVIRONMENT Conservative sober colours. Especially browns and fawns. No preoccupation with clothes, fashions or style. Little sense of 'what goes with what'. Workplace is sterile and efficient. Generally has graphs on walls, manuals and reference texts in bookshelves. Prefer to deal with people from behind a desk, which is neat and efficient at all times. There is a place for everything and everything in its place. Almost everything they buy could be described as 'conservative and safe'.

LIFE THEMES 'I'm still yet to be convinced that two plus two really makes four'.

MAJOR DRIVING FORCES Security through set procedure, facts, data; law and order. Procedural habits.

NATURAL HABITAT Low-risk environments such as the public service, financial institutions, law, accounting, computer programming, scientific research. Anywhere there are high levels of predictability and low entrepreneurial skills needed.

STRENGTHS   Diligent, accurate, systematic, persistent, organised, precise. Upholder of rules and set procedures. Objective and analytical. Cautious in actions and decisions. Good problem-solving and thinking skills. Self-disciplined. Follows directives.

SHORTCOMINGS   Stiff, picky, righteous. Over reliant on rules and procedures, data and information collection. Loner. Low risk-taker. Slow at making decisions. Slow to delegate.

UNDER STRESS   Under stress, particularly when forced to make a quick decision, the Owl will avoid. When under stress, the Owl takes flight.

TO BE MORE EFFECTIVE   To be more effective the Owl needs to be less critical, moralistic and stuffy. Less picky and detail oriented. They need to be a little more flexible in their thinking. Accept a few more risks. They need to try taking the first approach more often rather than analysing a situation to death. They need to speed up their decision-making, especially if they want to influence faster-moving people. They can be seen by some as a pain in the neck when it comes to detail. They can also appear dull and boring. They need more respect for who they are, rather than what they can do. They need to remember that life itself is risky - none of us is going to get out of it alive! They need to try taking a few more risks.

BOTTOM LINE   Owls are deep thinkers, quiet and withdrawn, with special skills which lead them to roles which require high reasoning and analytical skills.

DESCRIPTIONS AT A GLANCE

PEACOCK: *THE TALKER*

Confident	Optimistic
Outgoing	Carefree
Talkative	Spontaneous
Invigorating	Risk-taker
Enthusiastic	Friendly

ANIMATED & DRAMATIC

- ❖ Likes the spotlight
- ❖ Fast-paced
- ❖ Talks before listening
- ❖ People before tasks

DOVE: *THE FEELER*

Calm	Peaceful
Loyal	Practical
Dependable	Friendly
Patient	Passive
Serene	Stable

MODEST & CARING

- ❖ Wants to be supportive
- ❖ Calmer-paced
- ❖ Listens before talking
- ❖ People before tasks

EAGLE: *THE DOER*

Confident	Disciplined
Decisive	Direct
Loner	Forceful
Determined	Competitive
Productive	Controlled

DIRECT & BOSSY

- ❖ Likes being the boss
- ❖ Fast-paced
- ❖ Talks before listening
- ❖ Tasks before people

OWL: *THE THINKER*

Calm	Efficient
Systematic	Conservative
Reserved	Diplomatic
Analytical	Predictable
Perfectionist	Diligent

RESERVED & QUIET

- ❖ Wants to be right
- ❖ Calmer-paced
- ❖ Listens before talking
- ❖ Tasks before people

STRENGTHS AND WEAKNESSES

Along with our strengths, or perhaps because of them, we also carry our inbuilt weaknesses. Our strengths and our shortcomings are different sides of the same coin. What makes us strong can also make us weak. Our weaknesses are simply our strengths which have been taken too far, past the point of balance.

THE PEACOCK The Peacock's strength lies in their natural ability to be fast-paced and to verbalise their thoughts in a confident and persuasive way. But take that strength too far, past the point of balance, and the Peacock can appear to be a 'loudmouth', pushy show-off who opens his or her mouth to change feet!

THE EAGLE The Eagle's strength lies in his or her ability to control things, to get things done in a given time, to take charge of a situation, to be the boss. But take that strength past the point of balance, and Eagles can be seen as bossy, dictatorial impatient first cousins to Adolf Hitler and Attila the Hun!

THE DOVE The Doves' strength lies in their pleasant and compliant nature; their ability to be supportive, to calm troubled waters, to achieve peace at almost any price. But take that strength too far, and the Dove can be perceived as over-compliant, unmotivated, weak and 'wishy-washy', and to be eaten for breakfast by the Eagles!

THE OWL The Owls' strength lies in their ability to weigh up all the pros and cons, to get things right, their accuracy, their logic and reasoning powers. But take that natural ability too far, and the Owl can be seen as a deathly dull and boring person who can never make a decision. And who finds it impossible to order something from a menu in under half an hour!

IN SEARCH OF BALANCE

To develop or strengthen our weaknesses we need to keep our strengths in check and in balance.

The following is a list of individual strengths and the corresponding weaknesses that those strengths could become when taken too far. It may be worth doing a stocktake of how others may see us when we take our strengths too far.

STRENGTHS AND WEAKNESSES

THE PEACOCK

Confident	Egocentric
Talkative	Loud
Persuasive	Pushy
Enthusiastic	Excitable
Optimistic	Dreamer
Carefree	Careless
Outgoing	Intrusive

THE DOVE

Calm	Inactive
Loyal	Dependent
Patient	Unsure
Serene	Complacent
Practical	Conservative
Passive	Unmotivated
Helpful	Compliant

THE EAGLE

Decisive	Unbending
Independent	Loner
Determined	Autocratic
Productive	Workaholic
Disciplined	Bossy
Direct	Tactless
Forceful	Uncaring

THE OWL

Careful	Inactive
Systematic	Inflexible
Restrained	Withdrawn
Analytical	Indecisive
Efficient	Officious
Predictable	Boring
Diligent	Fussy

No matter how silly it may look
to you, remember that it
always makes sense
to the person
doing it.

MAJOR MOTIVATING FORCES

Our actions and our words will invariably reflect our driving needs. Whenever we open our mouths it is to fulfil a need that is important to us. We deal in our own 'emotional currency.'

We all have an 'emotional currency', those things that are important to us. And like money, we all need to deal in our own currency so that we can live and feel comfortable with ourselves.

Emotional currencies are our emotional needs. They are our major driving forces. They are the things that motivate us. They lie at the heart of why we do the things we do. They help make us who we are. They are our reasons to exist. They lie at the heart of what makes us tick. In fact, they are what make us tick.

People do things for their reasons, not yours, and they always will. When we know another's major driving force, their reasons, their emotional currency, then we can understand what makes them do the things they do.

By gaining this understanding we can have the ability to move into another's world. To understand their emotional currency, what drives them, gives us the key to their world.

When we can align our propositions and ideas to appeal to another's reasons, to their driving forces, then we have learnt the secret of motivation. (The root meaning of the words 'motivate', 'motive', and 'emotion' is 'to move.' Hence the truth in the axiom: 'Logic only makes me think, it is emotions that make me act.')

As human beings, we each strive to have our emotional needs fulfilled. Our emotional needs are the motives, the reasons, for doing what we do. Tell me what I want to hear and I'll follow you anywhere!

The following are the major motivational forces of the four basic styles.

MAJOR MOTIVATING FORCES

THE PEACOCK

Wants popularity and applause. Wants to be complimented, thanked and applauded for who they are and what they can do. Wants to be recognised for what they have or will achieve.
Wants to be famous.

THE DOVE

Wants the security of belonging. Wants to be a supportive and valued part of a group. Wants to be appreciated as an important member of the team. Wants to live in harmony.
Wants to be needed.

THE EAGLE

Wants authority and power. Wants to have control. Wants to have the freedom to get quick results. Wants to make things happen. Wants to bring about change
Wants to be the boss.

THE OWL

Wants to have security through facts, figures and systems. Wants to work and live within set patterns, habits, and laid down procedures. Wants to be right before taking any action.
Wants to have predictability.

CLASHING PERSONALITIES

Most of the people we find hard to get along with normally look out of a diagonal window.

We tend to see the weaknesses in our diagonal opposites, rather than their strengths.

It was Robbie Burns, the Scottish poet, who talked about the gift of seeing ourselves as others see us. The following illustration helps us to do that.

Look at that boring fussy person. Wouldn't get excited if there was a fire in the building. What a pain in the ... !

Look at that overpowering bossy Hitler. How would you like living with that!

THE PEACOCK

THE DOVE

THE EAGLE

THE OWL

What a wimp! Weak and wishy-washy. No initiative A real doormat. No motivation, that's the problem.

What a loud-mouthed show-off! Frivolous, flamboyant and a real pain in the ... !

Criticism is another way of saying *"Why can't you be more like me?"*

PEACOCKS Because Peacocks are fast, warm and friendly, they usually have little patience with their opposites the Owls who are slower, cooler and analytical.

EAGLES Because Eagles are fast, cool and like being in control, they usually have little patience with their opposites the Doves who are slower, warm and supportive.

DOVES   Because Doves are slower, warm and friendly, they usually have problems with their opposites the Eagles who are fast, cool and bossy.

OWLS   Because Owls are slower, cool and analytical, they usually have difficulties with their opposites the Peacocks who are fast, warm and friendly.

When I'm with you I feel relaxed
enough to be me.

Relationships are about giving people
the opportunity to be themselves, warts
and all, when they are with you.

A true relationship starts when
the other person's needs become
as important as your own.

SECTION TWO

RELATIONSHIP STRATEGIES

AT HOME, AT WORK AND AT PLAY

HOW TO GET ALONG WITH THE PEACOCK

Peacocks are outgoing, friendly, optimistic and happy-go-lucky and will be in anything that looks like fun, especially where other people are involved.

Good-natured and easygoing, they are great talkers with a repertoire of the latest jokes, which you will hear whether you want to or not!

Prone to say exactly what they are thinking at the time, they often have to open their mouth to change feet.

Enthusiastic, talkative and optimistic, their enthusiasm is often seen by some as flamboyance.

Imaginative, innovative and entrepreneurial, they have a natural ability to persuade others to their ideas.

Ambitious and adventurous, they tend to jump in feet first, ignoring the details (which they hate) only to come unstuck when the nitty-gritty details raise their ugly heads.

Being optimistic and imaginative, they often get caught up in the excitement of an idea, but can just as quickly get bored with it. They are great starters but poor finishers. They also tend to try and do a million things at a time, with obvious consequences. Nothing is ever quite finished!

They are risk-takers, both professionally and socially. They have no trouble talking to people, including strangers on the street. Things are done on the spur of the moment, 'If it feels good, do it'.

Intuitive rather than practical, emotional rather than intellectual, they have temper outbursts which usually include lots of noise and drama.

They find it hard to be punctual (time is elastic) and find structure and procedure stifling. They also hate doing paperwork.

They like getting attention and being recognised by others. They strive for some form of achievement that will give them recognition, fame and popularity. These are the things that make the Peacock tick.

Flashy, bright coloured cars (especially red) and designer label clothes were invented for Peacocks!

LIVING AND WORKING WITH THE PEACOCK Because the Peacock is a social and showy bird who strives for acknowledgment and recognition, it is important to applaud and recognise them for who they are and what they can do. The Peacock lives on compliments and 'Thank you's'. They can never get enough of either. Give them constant praise and recognition.

They hate being 'locked in' to repetitive and non-changing environments. They want to be where the action is.

Let them do most of the talking. Give them creative freedom to get a job done. But also make sure you give them firm guidelines and time frames to operate within, otherwise things can get out of hand.

Give them freedom from structure, use their ability to create ideas, their verbalising and motivating skills, their ability to contact people, their ability to make favourable impressions, and their desire to help others. Constantly praise them and give them the spotlight. When you do all these things, you will find that you have unleashed a tireless dynamo.

RELATING TO THE PEACOCK Let them do most of the talking. Keep the conversation moving. Don't get bogged down in details. Appeal to their ego. Recognise their importance. Be warm and friendly. Make people the talking point, especially them. They think in pictures. Use expressive words, paint word pictures. Be entertaining. Avoid being conservative or analytical. When making a proposal to them, talk in concepts and results. Avoid analytical detail otherwise you'll lose their interest. They think fast and decide fast. They are impulsive.

MOTIVATING THE PEACOCK Remember, Peacocks strive for recognition and applause, especially public recognition. They want to be the centre of attention. They want to stand out from the crowd. They want fame, popularity and lots of applause and praise. If they don't get it at home or at work, they'll use their energy to get it elsewhere; by joining organisations, clubs, being elected to the council (and becoming president or mayor), or pursuing other positions which will give them the recognition and status they crave.

HOT BUTTON Show them how you can help them achieve fame and recognition.

STRATEGY Appeal to their ego. Let them be the centre of attention. Recognise and praise often. Applause is worth more than money. Show them how you can help them to achieve a goal which will bring them recognition and they will follow you anywhere!

Keep conversations moving and interesting, unless you are talking about them! Don't bog them down with details or paperwork. They are fast moving, action-centred people. Communicate with them in the same way. They watch three shows on TV at once. The remote control was invented for them to keep them interested! That should give you some idea of how they like their conversations to flow.

DEFENCE MECHANISM Their natural defence reaction is to attack with lots of emotion, noise and drama. Everyone within earshot will hear them. But their emotional outbursts are short lived. Usually, within a short time after the explosion they normally want to be friends again as if nothing happened. Which in their opinion it didn't!

41

RECREATION In sports and recreation you will find Peacocks wherever they can be the centre of attention, particularly doing physically daring and risky things. They love displaying their talents with bravado, as long as someone is watching. The bigger the audience the better. They are definitely not quiet achievers!

RELATIONSHIP STRATEGIES: DO'S AND DONT'S

DO'S
+ Do be enthusiastic and optimistic when around them.
+ Do accept the fact that they like talking about themselves.
+ Do let them do most of the talking, they will anyway.
+ Do be an interested and attentive audience.
+ Do keep them on track by interjecting with questions.
+ Do understand that they exaggerate everything.
+ Do let them be the centre of attention.
+ Do recognise and comment on their ability.
+ Do give them lots of praise and compliments.
+ Do keep your conversation moving and interesting.
+ Do understand that they are emotional.
+ Do appreciate they like to touch and cuddle.
+ Do have a sense of humour when you are with them.
+ Do appreciate that they crack jokes to ease their tension.
+ Do help them to achieve success and popularity.
+ Do encourage their aspirations and goals.
+ Do appreciate they like to have fun.
+ Do let them feel free to use their imagination.
+ Do understand that they work in high spurts of energy.
+ Do accept the fact that to them time is like elastic.
+ Do accept the fact that they are unorganised.
+ Do accept that when they're down, they're really down.
+ Do appreciate that they are terrible at handling money.
+ Do help them to use logic and analytical judgement.

DON'TS
+ Don't expect them to take a logical approach.
+ Don't expect them to take things lying down.
+ Don't lock them into repetitious tasks and environments.
+ Don't expect them to be good listeners.
+ Don't expect them to do good things without constant praise.
+ Don't expect them to be a quiet part of the crowd, or team.
+ Don't expect them to work well without recognition.
+ Don't bog them down with details.
+ Don't criticise them about being impractical with money, they already know they are.

- ◆ Don't criticise them about their dreams and ambitions.
- ◆ Don't expect them to let you have the last word.
- ◆ Don't expect them to be a homebody.

SQUARE PEGS IN SQUARE HOLES

Because of the Peacocks' people-orientation and constant search for applause and recognition they are naturals as:

- ◆ actors
- ◆ entertainers
- ◆ speakers
- ◆ trainers

- ◆ politicians
- ◆ salespeople
- ◆ entrepreneurs
- ◆ public relations people

SQUARE PEGS IN ROUND HOLES

Also, because of the Peacocks' natural orientation and needs, they are not good at jobs which call for:

- ◆ compiling analytical data
- ◆ analytical judgement
- ◆ unchanging and structured routine work
- ◆ little opportunity for personal recognition
- ◆ the necessity to work alone
- ◆ little chance to display talents
- ◆ little opportunity to deal with people
- ◆ being a quiet part of a team

The more the above elements are involved in the job, the more stressed the Peacock will feel. You will have a fish out of water. You will have a Peacock trying to do an Owl's job and messing it up. It can be compared to having a natural footballer trying to play the harp!

IN A NUTSHELL

The Peacock is extroverted, talkative and friendly, with a powerful desire to be recognised by others for the skills and talents they possess. They crave fame, popularity, a good reputation, and constant appreciation. Because with recognition comes security, and with security comes satisfaction. These are the things that motivate the Peacock. These are the things that make the Peacock tick.

HOW TO GET ALONG WITH THE DOVE

The Dove is shy, friendly and sensitive. They are rarely, if ever, impulsive or demonstrative. Everything is done in moderation, low key, and low profile.

Doves are warm and caring people who are concerned about the welfare of others. Doves avoid trouble, conflict and aggressive people like the plague. They are highly sensitive to threats, both real and imagined. They are flighters rather than fighters, settlers rather than pioneers. They keep the home fires burning.

Doves find social interaction risky and threatening. Strangers are to be avoided. They have a close network of comfortable and non-threatening friends and like to stick within that circle, at home and at work.

Steady, reliable and predictable, they make conscientious workers, loyal supporters and sincere friends with a willing and sympathetic ear for whatever ails you. Being the centre of attention - being in the spotlight - embarrasses the heck out of them. It is against everything they stand for, which is to fit in, to be part of the crowd, to not make waves, to live a quiet and predictable life.

Doves are set in their ways. They rarely show displays of enthusiasm or spontaneity. They just get on with things in their own time and in their own calm and pleasant way. Hurrying them only upsets and flusters them because it represents a threat to their normal routines and habits, which in turn is a threat to their sense of security.

Doves are good at hiding what they are thinking and feeling. They are extremely sensitive and their feelings are easily wounded. More intuitive than practical, more compassionate than pragmatic, they can be incredibly stubborn though for no apparent reason.

They are pleasant, caring and tactful. They strive for stability through belonging, acceptance, friendship, affection and love. To the Dove, life is meaningful when these things are fulfilled. These are the things that make the Dove tick.

Mini-vans and Toyota Corollas were invented for the Doves. With a mini-van all the family can pile in. And Toyota Corollas? Well they're not flashy and almost everyone's got one!

LIVING AND WORKING WITH THE DOVE Doves are warm timid people who are fiercely loyal to the people they care about. They make supportive and loving partners, and great team members.

They need lots of reassuring that they're needed and appreciated. They can be hurt easily and should be treated with TLC, which they themselves give to others in abundance. When hurt, they will become quiet and withdrawn. They fly quickly from any hint of conflict or aggression. They thrive in a warm and friendly atmosphere.

They dislike any disruption to the normal pattern of things. They are creatures of habit, both in things and people. This helps give them their sense of security and belonging.

Under pressure they may appear to agree rather than face conflict or the loss of a relationship, but will reverse once away from the situation. They will buy today and send back tomorrow. The saying, 'I just can't say no', was invented for the Dove.

Don't expect the Dove to make decisions or initiate action. They prefer to follow rather than lead.

RELATING TO THE DOVE Be warm, caring and friendly with the Dove. Don't try and rush them into anything. They don't like any changes to the scheme of things. Constancy equals comfort to the Dove.

Reduce any risk of sudden changes when dealing with the Dove. If change needs to take place, then introduce it slowly in a non-threatening way. Give them plenty of time to think about it first.

Don't be pushy or demanding, otherwise you will get a 'yes' that really means a 'no'. Don't confuse the issue with too many choices. Get agreement progressively.

Show personal interest. Be prepared to talk about little personal things that may not seem relevant to you or to the point of the conversation.

Give personal assurances and guarantees. Doves are comfortable and pleasant people. And that's just how they like to be dealt with.

MOTIVATING THE DOVE Remember, the Dove strives for the security of belonging. They want to be a supportive part of a group. They have no wish to stand out from the crowd. They are the ultimate team members. The welfare of others, and having their friendship, is worth more than money to the Dove. Talk and show them that they belong, and are an important part of the group, and they'll follow you anywhere!

HOT BUTTON Show them that they are needed and an important member of the group, both for who they are as well as what they can do and what they can contribute.

STRATEGY Appeal to their sense of 'belonging', their importance as an integral part of the group. Don't rush change. Change of any sort threatens their security. And don't force prominence on to them. Don't single them out. Strangers and new social situations are also seen as threatening. Play down the risks. Keep conversations warm and friendly. Talk about people rather than analytical detail or facts and figures. Be relaxed, slow and easy. Let them feel comfortable and not rushed. Offer lots of reassurance.

DEFENCE MECHANISM Their natural reaction to threat is to submit and go quiet. Defence is in submission. But don't let this fool you. The Dove can be incredibly stubborn (but quiet) when they dig their heels in.

RECREATION Find a team or a group of people and you will find a Dove in there being supportive. If not, you will find them in some intense, but alone, activity doing for others: dressmaking, cooking, making or repairing toys, running the kids around to sport or dancing lessons. Their recreation can be described in the phrase, 'Doing for others'. They are not competitive, and get involved in sports for the activity and social aspects rather than to compete and win at all costs. They are the hard and seemingly tireless workers on amateur sporting club committees. But don't ask them to sell raffle tickets. They hate it, because that means they have to approach strangers, or worse, be pushy!

RELATIONSHIP STRATEGIES: DO'S AND DON'TS

The Dove is quiet, friendly and shy, and seeks acceptance as a supportive and needed member of a group.

DO'S
- Do be warm, friendly and sensitive.
- Do be patient and supportive.
- Do reassure their sense of belonging.
- Do communicate in a slow, sincere manner.
- Do give plenty of time when introducing change.
- Do give clear descriptions and expectations of tasks.
- Do provide a happy and stable environment.
- Do give help in making decisions.
- Do try to eliminate any perceived risks of change.
- Do give help in starting new projects or tasks.
- Do understand that they are emotional and sentimental.
- Do establish yourself as a good and loyal friend.
- Do be kind and understanding.
- Do be calm, peaceful and relaxed.
- Do accept the fact that people's feelings are more important to them than getting the job done.
- Do understand that they won't speak up for themselves.
- Do show that you can be a shoulder to lean on.
- Do give them appreciation for who they are, as well as what they can do.

DON'TS
- Don't expect them to stand out from the crowd.
- Don't expect them to tell other people what to do.
- Don't rush them into anything.
- Don't change their normal patterns of doing things.

- Don't expect them to do many things at the same time.
- Don't expect them to be comfortable in a public situation.
- Don't expect them to make decisions or take risks.
- Don't expect them to deal with unfriendly people.
- Don't expect them to live or work in a pressure environment.
- Don't expect them to sell anything.
- Don't expect them to take the initiative.
- Don't expect them to work with broad guidelines, be specific.
- Don't expect them to work alone or unaided.
- Don't expect them to be competitive.
- Don't praise or flatter in public, this is embarrassing.
- Don't criticise others, especially their friends.
- Don't ever question their loyalty.
- Don't criticise them for being too casual.

SQUARE PEGS IN SQUARE HOLES

Because of the Doves' strong people-orientation, caring and compassion, they are naturals as:

- social workers
- religious workers
- customer-service
- support staff
- counsellors
- nurses
- parents
- teachers

SQUARE PEGS IN ROUND HOLES

Also, because of the Doves' natural orientation and needs, they are not good at jobs which call for:

- telling other people what to do
- making decisions
- taking the initiative
- dealing with aggressive people
- selling or promoting
- the necessity to work alone
- broad job guidelines
- low job security
- salary based on performance: commissions
- unpredictable situations

The more these things are involved in a job, the more stressed the Dove will feel.

You will have the wrong person doing the wrong job. You will have one very uptight Dove trying to do what they're not good at. It can be compared to having a champion tennis player trying valiantly to be a boxer!

IN A NUTSHELL

The Dove is warm, friendly, shy and caring with a powerful desire for stability through belonging. They crave acceptance, affection, friendship and love. Only then is life meaningful. Because with acceptance comes security, and with security comes satisfaction. These are the things that motivate the Dove. That is what makes the Dove tick.

HOW TO GET ALONG WITH THE EAGLE

The Eagle is a no-nonsense person who displays a certain coolness and aloofness which always keeps you at arm's length.

They are always in a hurry, showing a detached sense of urgency, and are usually preoccupied with something that's more important than talking to you.

Self-assured and self-opinionated, they are a law unto themselves. They can be seen by some as abrupt, aggressive, tactless and totally independent.

Their world seems to revolve around them and what they can get out of it. Eagles are highly competitive. They hate losing, and that includes coming second.

Impatient and critical, they hate waiting - for anything: in queues, at restaurants, anywhere. They want everything straight away. 'Time is money'.

Eagles will not suffer fools and will avoid them like the plague. And the Eagle seems to come across many fools in the course of the day. Tolerance and patience are not the Eagle's long suits.

They are impulsive decision-makers who make decisions to suit themselves. 'I'm all right Jack, stuff you' often seems to be the message they are sending out to those around them.

They are also not known for having a keen sense of humour. When they do make a witty remark it generally has plenty of sting to it and is normally directed at a specific target. More practical than intuitive, more materialistic than compassionate, they are generally totally oblivious to how stinging their off-handed remarks can be to others.

They are confident and radiate personal power. They strive for power over others through achievement of position, prestige, status or sheer dominance of personality. It is this striving for power and the need for results that makes the Eagle tick.

LIVING AND WORKING WITH THE EAGLE   As far as the Eagle is concerned, there are only two ways to do something. Their way and the wrong way!

They like to be in control at all times. To say they are strong willed is an understatement.

They live and thrive on results and being in charge. They love a challenge and the chance it gives to prove their ability to get the job done. They live on getting results and bringing about changes in 'the way things have always been done'.

They are the perfect agents for bringing about change in a static or arthritic organisation. But they tend to break bones rather than massage them!

For somebody looking for a 'strong' leader or partner they are the answer to a dream. But be prepared to give them the authority and freedom to be the boss; if you don't, you'll feel the sharpness of their talons.

RELATING TO THE EAGLE Be quick and to the point with the Eagle. Don't beat around the bush. Unless you are making sense to them, they will either turn off, become short and impatient, or both. Stick to the point with them.

Avoid 'small talk', details and irrelevancies. Give them the basic facts and the 'bottom line' only.

They don't like being told to do anything. They do the telling. Ask the Eagles, don't tell them.

They want to be in charge. Let them do most of the talking because they hate listening. Show them results. Don't give them excuses. Results are all that matter. Time is at a premium. Be definite, specific, clear, brief and to the point. Deal in facts not emotions. And always do what you say you will do.

Recognise their ability, power and authority, and show them how to get quick results and you'll have no trouble with Eagles.

MOTIVATING THE EAGLE Eagles are no-nonsense people who like to get results, without messing around. And they like the freedom and power to make the decisions that get them those results. They want to be the boss in everything they do. Give them a challenge and the freedom to get it done their way and watch them go!

HOT BUTTON Give them the authority to take control.

STRATEGY Appeal to their sense of authority. Let them take charge. Show them how to get results in the quickest way and they'll always listen to you. Bog them down in detailed explanations and excuses and you'll see them become impatient and turn off.

Keep conversations quick and to the point. Avoid small talk and personal matters. Talk in short-hand! Ask questions rather than make long-winded statements.

DEFENCE MECHANISM Their natural reaction is to attack. Either with sarcasm or becoming authoritative and bossy, using logic and facts in an autocratic way.

RECREATION The Eagle is not a spectator. Rather than look, they want to be involved and getting results. Winning. They prefer one-person pursuits such as sailing, tennis, racing, etc., in fact anything where they are not just a member of a team, unless they are captain or the coach, or both! Like everything else, they 'play' very seriously. Eagles are extremely competitive animals.

They play everything to win. When not at competitive recreation they will either be at work or doing something else which gets a result.

RELATIONSHIP STRATEGIES: DO'S AND DON'TS

The Eagle is quick-paced, dominant and assertive and wants to be in control of you, themselves and the situation.

DO'S
- Do let them be, or appear to be, in control.
- Do keep conversations brief and to the point.
- Do let them make the decisions.
- Do appreciate that discipline rules their lives.
- Do let them be the leader, or think they are.
- Do help them to achieve authority and status.
- Do be emotionally controlled.
- Do show you have an independent nature.
- Do be a good listener.
- Do be decisive.
- Do stick to positives.
- Do let them feel free to get results.
- Do accept the fact that their career comes first.
- Do understand that they are highly competitive.

DON'TS
- Don't expect them to be part of the crowd.
- Don't expect them to be good listeners.
- Don't offer long-winded explanations or excuses.
- Don't expect them to be patient.
- Don't expect them to explain their decisions and actions.
- Don't expect them to work in unchanging environments.
- Don't expect them to sacrifice themselves for others.
- Don't expect them to become involved with analytical detail.
- Don't expect them to be timid in the face of argument.
- Don't talk too much, especially when they want to talk.
- Don't be timid with them, they see it as a weakness.
- Don't beat around the bush with them.
- Don't try and be intimate, avoid emotional appeals.
- Don't ever break a promise or commitment to them.
- Don't indulge in long telephone conversations.
- Don't be upset by their sarcasm or knife-edged comments.
- Don't expect them to be compassionate, or cry in sad movies.
- Don't try and boss them around.
- Don't expect them to be service-orientated.
- Don't ever tell them lies, even white ones.
- Don't be possessive or clingy.
- Don't try to lay down rules.

SQUARE PEGS IN SQUARE HOLES

Because of the Eagles' strong task-orientation and constant need to be in control they are naturals as:

- military leaders
- project managers
- change agents
- union leaders

- police
- editors
- directors
- politicians

SQUARE PEGS IN ROUND HOLES

Also, because of the Eagles' natural orientation and needs, they are not good at jobs which call for:

- structured and routine tasks
- being a supportive part of a team
- little input into the decision-making process
- little chance of promotion
- little opportunity to exert authority
- long-term patience
- constant contact with the public

The more the above elements are involved in the job, the more stressed the Eagle will feel. You will have trouble on your hands. You will have an Eagle doing a Dove's job. It can be likened to having a natural soccer player being forced to play the piano!

IN A NUTSHELL

The Eagle is fast, dominant and result-orientated with a burning desire to be independent and powerful as perceived by both themselves and others. They crave status, authority and respect. Because with power and respect comes security, and with security comes satisfaction. These are the things that motivate the Eagle. These are the things that make the Eagle tick.

HOW TO GET ALONG WITH THE OWL

The Owl is conservative, reserved, detached and aloof, and likes to do things alone and uninterrupted. They are pessimistic and cautious, and have an obsessive desire for detail.

They are facts and figures people whose lives are structured around sameness and predictability.

Owls are restrained and unbending when it comes to rules, regulations and accepted ways of doing things.

They are exasperatingly thorough and obsessively meticulous. They are intolerant of change and new ideas. They are wooden in facial expression (poker faced) and take life very seriously indeed.

Indecisive and unadventurous, they are critical and suspicious of anyone who tries to do things differently to the normal scheme of things.

They like detail work, doing a bit at a time. They prefer doing small bits of the big picture. They tend to become nervous and fretful under pressure, particularly the pressure of having to make a decision.

Whilst extremely critical of others, Owls can't handle criticism themselves. When it is offered, they become quietly irritable, are prone to sulking, withdraw and go away by themselves where they can shut you out.

They are logical, exacting and precise. They see things in black and white. Their confidence comes through having all the facts, although it is impossible to ever get enough! They strive to be right. They want 100 per cent accuracy. They want perfection.

Owls make dependable backroom people who will not waver from established procedure and standards. Loyal to socially accepted standards, they have a strong sense of duty, are hard working, and meticulously accurate and precise.

They tend to have sophisticated calculators and digital watches with about twenty functions, including what time it is on Mars!

They strive to live in an orderly, structured and predictable world with no threats of change or disruption to the normal pattern of things.

LIVING AND WORKING WITH THE OWL The Owl is a solitary bird which prefers its own company. A quiet, deep thinker, the Owl prefers to think rather than talk. They prefer to 'do' something rather than waste their time on social activities and the other things which may seem 'enjoyable' to others. They have little time for idle chatter. Small talk and conversation is hard work.

The Owl prefers the security of the known, therefore sudden or abrupt changes without strong facts or reasons for the change are the Owl's major turn-off.

They need answers for everything.

The Owl deals in facts, not feelings. Owls rarely ask you how you feel, rather they will ask you what you're doing. They are inquisitive people who are more interested in 'what's being done rather than 'who' is doing it.

The Owl likes a predictable, secure and safe habitat that has little chance of risk and is high in rules, regulations, laws and established patterns and procedures.

Like everything else, they are cautious and conservative with their money. They give a dollar a very good home! Yet they will have no trouble spending a small fortune on sophisticated Hi-Fi equipment, or a whiz-bang computer.

They can be very critical when others don't measure up to their own standards. As a partner or co-worker the Owl can be seen as cool and distant. Don't expect too many displays of emotion from the Owl, or gossipy conversations.

RELATING TO THE OWL Take it slowly and stick to facts and logic. Be organised. Don't talk about emotions, feelings, or personal things. Give plenty of analytical and factual detail, the more the better.

Make sure it is on paper. If it is not on paper, it doesn't exist for the Owl.

Don't try and rush them into anything. They need time to think and contemplate. Try rushing Owls and you will see them become suspicious, negative and pessimistic and withdraw into their feathers. You will get a 'no' that could have been a 'yes' if you had given them more time to think about it.

Owls prefer to think and do only one thing at a time. Plant new ideas slowly and gradually, giving as much information, logic and reason as you can find to support the idea. Remember, change equals threat to the Owl.

If you're going to tell them a joke (which you shouldn't), make sure they know beforehand that it is a joke! A sense of humour is not one of the Owl's strongest points.

If you are trying to sell something to the Owl, keep in mind they are always looking for the 'catch', they will want to know about guarantees. The phrase, 'No risk, no problems', was not invented for the Owl - but the Volvo car was!

MOTIVATING THE OWL Remember, Owls are motivated through the security of 'being right'. They get comfort and safety from following set patterns (habits) and procedures. Rules and the accepted way of doing things are important as are facts, figures and data. Any change from the normal is seen as risky and threatening. They want to be right.

HOT BUTTON Show them how they can be right and safe with a minimum of risk.

STRATEGY Appeal to logic. Avoid emotional appeals. Stick to the facts. Show proof through information, research and data. Give evidence. Avoid small talk or anything of a personal nature. Progress the conversation in logical steps. Don't rush them. Give time for thought. Avoid suggesting sudden changes to the existing scheme of things. Give plenty of time for considering any changes that threaten their normal habits and procedures.

DEFENCE MECHANISM Their natural reaction is to withdraw from, or avoid the situation, or person, which is causing the discomfort. Their solitude and quietness can become acute.

RECREATION Obviously, the Owl is not a social creature. Their recreation can seem like work to others. Normally it takes the form of some intense and singular activity. They can often be found 'playing' with computers, electronic gadgetry or mechanical (predictable) things. They like 'making things' and have the patience of Job when it comes to detailed and intricate work. They are big readers, but rarely read fiction preferring instead to read to learn. Anything that they can do alone which involves thinking is attractive to the Owl. Owls can often be found in abundance in archery, pistol shooting, and chess clubs.

RELATIONSHIP STRATEGIES: DO'S AND DON'TS

The Owl is deliberate, slower-paced and conservative, and won't have a bar of anything different or risky.

DO'S
- Do be sensitive to their need for solitude.
- Do give them plenty of time to make decisions.
- Do offer facts and logic on paper.
- Do appreciate they would rather stay home than go out.
- Do give appreciation for what they can do, not who they are.
- Do communicate in a slower structured way.
- Do give plenty of time to think about and prepare for change.
- Do give precise and detailed instructions and expectations.
- Do be emotionally controlled.
- Do be fussy about details.
- Do take an intellectual approach.
- Do seek their advice on analytical matters.
- Do accept the fact that tasks come before people.
- Do respect their old-fashioned values.

DON'TS
- Don't try and push them into quick decisions.
- Don't suggest anything that may appear (to them) risky.
- Don't introduce any sudden changes to their set patterns.
- Don't expect them to take responsibility for others.
- Don't expect them to be a decision-maker.
- Don't expect them to be a leader.
- Don't expect them to do many things at the same time.

- Don't expect them to delegate important tasks.
- Don't expect them to take an unpopular stand.
- Don't expect any displays of emotion.
- Don't expect them to know what you want: be specific.
- Don't flatter them.
- Don't criticise them: for anything.
- Don't expect them to be optimistic.
- Don't expect them to be competitive.
- Don't appear disorganised to them.
- Don't exaggerate or appear extravagant.
- Don't give the impression that work is a game.
- Don't try to get too close.
- Don't try to persuade them into anything.
- Don't expect them to deal with the public.
- Don't come on too eager or enthusiastic.
- Don't touch or stand too close.
- Don't invade their privacy.
- Don't expect them to be partygoers or socialisers.

SQUARE PEGS IN SQUARE HOLES

Because of the Owls' strong task-orientation, meticulousness and constant need to be precise and accurate, they are naturals as:

- accountants
- computer programmers
- engineers
- bank managers
- researchers
- solicitors
- scientists
- professors

SQUARE PEGS IN ROUND HOLES

Also because of the Owls' natural orientation and needs, they are not good at jobs which call for:

- being responsible for others
- making quick decisions
- dealing with the public
- selling or promoting
- delegating tasks
- broad or vague job specifications
- a minimum of structure and procedure
- low job security
- unpredictable situations

The more the above elements are involved in the job, the more stressed the Owl will feel. You will have a fish very much out of water. You will have an Owl doing things they are just not good at. It could be compared to having a natural chess player being forced to play hockey!

IN A NUTSHELL

The Owl is conservative, quiet, detached and cool. They crave accuracy and perfectionism. They have a powerful desire to live in an orderly, structured and predictable world where there are no threats of change or disruption to their normal way of doing things. Because with structure and predictability comes security, and with security comes satisfaction. These are the things that motivate the Owl. These are the things that make the Owl tick.

THE PEACOCK AT A QUICK GLANCE

A TALKER.
Confident, friendly,
outgoing, witty, flamboyant,
dramatic, persuasive, animated,
expressive.
Heart over head.
Puts people before tasks.

WANTS
Popularity. To be the centre of attention. To get recognition and applause through achievement. Wants to be famous.

DOES NOT WANT
- To be just part of the crowd.
- To be ignored.
- To listen for any length of time.
- Jobs that offer no chance to show their talents.
- To work in a protected environment.
- Activities that are boring and repetitious.
- To work alone.

NEEDS
- The spotlight.
- To do most of the talking.
- Lots of praise and compliments.
- To be the centre of attention.
- Quick answers: no details.
- Fast-moving conversations.

WHEN RELATING
Make it fast, warm, friendly and animated. Let them do most of the talking. Let them have the spotlight. Give plenty of praise and recognition

NATURALS AT
Being in the public eye: acting, entertaining, selling, speaking, public relations, politics, etc.

THE DOVE AT A QUICK GLANCE

A FEELER.
shy, friendly,
sensitive, patient,
moderate, loyal, a listener,
supportive.
Heart over head.
Puts people before tasks.

WANTS
Love and friendship. To be a supportive and caring member of a small group or team. Wants to belong, to be needed.

DOES NOT WANT
+ To be different from anybody else.
+ To be the boss.
+ To be rushed into anything.
+ To deal with unfriendly people or situations.
+ To work under pressure.
+ To have to make decisions.
+ To work alone.

NEEDS
+ A stable and happy environment.
+ Precise instructions on how a job should be done.
+ Appreciation for their supportiveness.
+ Help in making decisions.
+ Friends and loved ones.
+ A willing ear.

WHEN RELATING
Make it slow, warm, friendly and sincere. Doves have an in-built antenna that can detect insincerity at a hundred paces.

NATURALS AT
Supporting roles: nursing, social work, counselling, parenting, customer-service roles etc.

THE EAGLE AT A QUICK GLANCE

A DOER.
Confident, controlled, dominant, assertive, fast, cool, decisive, impatient, controlling.
Head over heart.
Puts tasks before people.

WANTS
To be the boss. To take charge. To make things happen. The authority, power and freedom to get things done. Wants results.

DOES NOT WANT
◆ To be part of the crowd.
◆ To hear excuses.
◆ To deal with slower people.
◆ Jobs that offer no challenge.
◆ Jobs that offer no chance for advancement.
◆ To sacrifice themselves for others.
◆ Activities that offer no competitiveness.

NEEDS
◆ Quick answers: no details.
◆ Fast conversational exchanges.
◆ To be in control of what's happening.
◆ To be the one who makes the decisions.
◆ Quick moving environments.
◆ To be the boss in everything.

WHEN RELATING
Make it fast. Stick to the point. Bottom line only. No detail unless it is asked for. Give no excuses. Keep feelings out of it. Stick to the facts.

NATURALS AT
Being in control: military leaders, union leaders, project managers, police, security personnel etc.

THE OWL AT A QUICK GLANCE

A THINKER.
Quiet, cool, distant,
logical, conservative,
reserved, cautious,
analytical.
Head over heart.
Puts tasks before people.

WANTS
Facts and figures. Structure and systems. Set procedures. Law and order. Wants life to be predictable.

DOES NOT WANT
+ To take any risks.
+ To be rushed into anything.
+ Sudden changes from set patterns.
+ Changing home or work environments.
+ Displays of feelings and emotions.
+ Broad or undefined guidelines.
+ To make decisions.

NEEDS
+ Structure and systems.
+ Security of no sudden changes.
+ Plenty of facts and information.
+ Plenty of time to prepare for change.
+ Risks kept to an absolute minimum.
+ Precise instructions and job specifications.

WHEN RELATING
Take it slow. Keep it logical. Give plenty of information, facts, figures and evidence. Don't rush them. Keep feelings out of it.

NATURALS AT
Systematic accuracy: accountants, bank managers, engineers, scientists, computer programmers, researchers etc.

If you are going to do what
you have always done, then
you are going to be what you
have always been.

Understanding self is the
first real step towards
personal progress.

Until we understand and
truly see ourselves as we are,
we are unlikely to change.

SECTION THREE

QUESTIONNAIRE
AND PROFILES

NOTICE TO TRAINERS AND HUMAN
RESOURCE PROFESSIONALS

A reminder that it is a breach of copyright and illegal to use any of the materials contained in this book for professional purposes including the bird symbols to depict personality styles and this questionnaire.

The following questionnaire is my 'book version' of the Personality Profile. Far more accurate and comprehensive Profiles with personalized reports (Classic, Premium and JobFit) are available at our website www.tick.com.au. These are also available for use, under license to Human Resource professional to use in the workplace and schools.

Refer to the front of this book for details on how to become a licensed user of the 'What Makes People Tick' materials, or visit our website at www.tick.com.au

THE PERSONAL INSIGHT PROFILE

As I said at the start, it would be nonsense to suggest that we all fit neatly into one window.

Most of us possess differing degrees of all the four windows, and depending on the degree, these will influence, or bias, our perceptions and behaviour and our reactions to what life puts in front of us.

Some of us do perceive life from only one dominant window. But there are more of us who see life from two windows. And then there are those of us who tend to have a shared view from three windows.

This section is designed around a questionnaire and a scoring sheet that will help you ascertain your preferred windows. This is then followed by the profile descriptions of the different window combinations.

When doing the questionnaire for plotting your profile description, remember that it can only be as accurate as your answers. And your answers will only be as accurate as how well you know yourself.

Or how honest you can be with yourself!

ABOUT THE QUESTIONNAIRE

Over the next 2 pages (Pages 65 – 66) there are some lists of words. Tick the words on the lists which you think best describe you. Do not tick more than 40 or less than 20. There is no time limit to the questionnaire. But It will probably take you about 5 -10 minutes.

Avoid analysing each word to death. Your first gut-reaction to each question is normally the most accurate. There are no right or wrong answers.

As a guide to filling in the questionnaire, focus yourself on a particular environment, say a work situation or a social situation.

It is accepted that the world forces us to be different people at different times, but for the sake of this questionnaire, tick only what you feel comfortable being most of the time.

If you are in two minds on any question then leave it blank.

HELPFUL HINT If you find this process difficult to answer, perhaps you can get somebody you know, and can trust to be honest with you, to help you. Or alternatively, get this other person to complete the lists on Pages 67 – 68.

How I see myself

Tick the words on the lists below which you think best describe you. Do not tick more than 40 or less than 20. And be honest with yourself.

☐ outgoing	☐ caring
☐ outspoken	☐ passive
☐ enthusiastic	☐ calm
☐ motivating	☐ modest
☐ optimistic	☐ gentle
☐ flamboyant	☐ sincere
☐ charming	☐ helpful
☐ imaginative	☐ easy-going
☐ persuasive	☐ even tempered
☐ unselfconscious	☐ pleasant
☐ carefree	☐ friendly
☐ impulsive	☐ good listener
☐ talkative	☐ shy
☐ spontaneous	☐ sympathetic
☐ friendly	☐ supportive
☐ exaggerates	☐ trusting
☐ animated	☐ dependable
☐ humorous	☐ kind
☐ dramatic	☐ peaceful
☐ lively	☐ warm hearted
☐ excitable	☐ tolerant
☐ energetic	☐ unassuming
☐ visual	☐ sensitive
☐ entertaining	☐ co-operative

P ☐

D ☐

How I see myself

- ☐ forceful
- ☐ cool
- ☐ independent
- ☐ businesslike
- ☐ competitive
- ☐ critical
- ☐ assertive
- ☐ bold
- ☐ decisive
- ☐ self-reliant
- ☐ efficient
- ☐ bossy
- ☐ impatient
- ☐ blunt
- ☐ productive
- ☐ workaholic
- ☐ unbending
- ☐ decisive
- ☐ tough
- ☐ determined
- ☐ ambitious
- ☐ domineering
- ☐ strong-willed
- ☐ aggressive

E

- ☐ conservative
- ☐ analytical
- ☐ practical
- ☐ reliable
- ☐ quiet
- ☐ stable
- ☐ detached
- ☐ systematic
- ☐ predictable
- ☐ perfectionist
- ☐ reserved
- ☐ loner
- ☐ unemotional
- ☐ pessimistic
- ☐ careful
- ☐ fussy
- ☐ stiff
- ☐ precise
- ☐ patient
- ☐ diplomatic
- ☐ efficient
- ☐ restrained
- ☐ unsociable
- ☐ indecisive

O

Now add up the totals in each column to reveal your prefered and dominant styles. The highest score is your most dominant style.

How others see myself

Get someone to tick the words on the lists below which you think best describe you. Do not tick more than 40 or less than 20. And be honest – I can take it!

- ☐ outgoing
- ☐ outspoken
- ☐ enthusiastic
- ☐ motivating
- ☐ optimistic
- ☐ flamboyant
- ☐ charming
- ☐ imaginative
- ☐ persuasive
- ☐ unselfconscious
- ☐ carefree
- ☐ impulsive
- ☐ talkative
- ☐ spontaneous
- ☐ friendly
- ☐ exaggerates
- ☐ animated
- ☐ humorous
- ☐ dramatic
- ☐ lively
- ☐ excitable
- ☐ energetic
- ☐ visual
- ☐ entertaining

- ☐ caring
- ☐ passive
- ☐ calm
- ☐ modest
- ☐ gentle
- ☐ sincere
- ☐ helpful
- ☐ easy-going
- ☐ even tempered
- ☐ pleasant
- ☐ friendly
- ☐ good listener
- ☐ shy
- ☐ sympathetic
- ☐ supportive
- ☐ trusting
- ☐ dependable
- ☐ kind
- ☐ peaceful
- ☐ warm hearted
- ☐ tolerant
- ☐ unassuming
- ☐ sensitive
- ☐ co-operative

P

D

How others see myself

☐ forceful	☐ conservative
☐ cool	☐ analytical
☐ independent	☐ practical
☐ businesslike	☐ reliable
☐ competitive	☐ quiet
☐ critical	☐ stable
☐ assertive	☐ detached
☐ bold	☐ systematic
☐ decisive	☐ predictable
☐ self-reliant	☐ perfectionist
☐ efficient	☐ reserved
☐ bossy	☐ loner
☐ impatient	☐ unemotional
☐ blunt	☐ pessimistic
☐ productive	☐ careful
☐ workaholic	☐ fussy
☐ unbending	☐ stiff
☐ decisive	☐ precise
☐ tough	☐ patient
☐ determined	☐ diplomatic
☐ ambitious	☐ efficient
☐ domineering	☐ restrained
☐ strong-willed	☐ unsociable
☐ aggressive	☐ indecisive

E

O

Thank you for helping me see myself as others see me. I'll let you know later whether or not I'm happy with it!

A LITTLE STORY

Before adding up your scores and heading to the next section, I would like to tell a little story...please read it and do a quick reflection on your answers.

I had a lady in a training course with people who all had similar job roles but had not met before. When introducing herself, she used phrases such as "I love my husband...." And, "My baby is most important to me..." And, "I have a small group of my long standing best friends..."

She was screaming **Dove** to me, and she was a lovely person as I got to know her better.

When she completed the questionnaire she had ticked so many in the Eagle list she came out as an **Extreme Eagle**.

She read her profile, and looking distressed, said, "This says I am really hard and nasty!" To which I replied, "Well you answered the questions!"

She wasn't happy with her profile, but when we analysed her answers, she had been thinking at the time that she needed to tick those words "because that's what her boss wanted to hear". So she wasn't being honest with herself – she answered to please her boss – how very Dove-like.

My point is that you will get the most by being honest with yourself – no one else.

YOUR PROFILE AT A GLANCE

Now plot your scores on the diagonal lines on the graph below and connect up the points to form a rough kite shape. Wherever most of the kite shape is pointing should generally describe your personality when you are in your comfort zone. Then refer to the next section for a more detailed description of your style. Note - scores above 20, plot at 20 only.

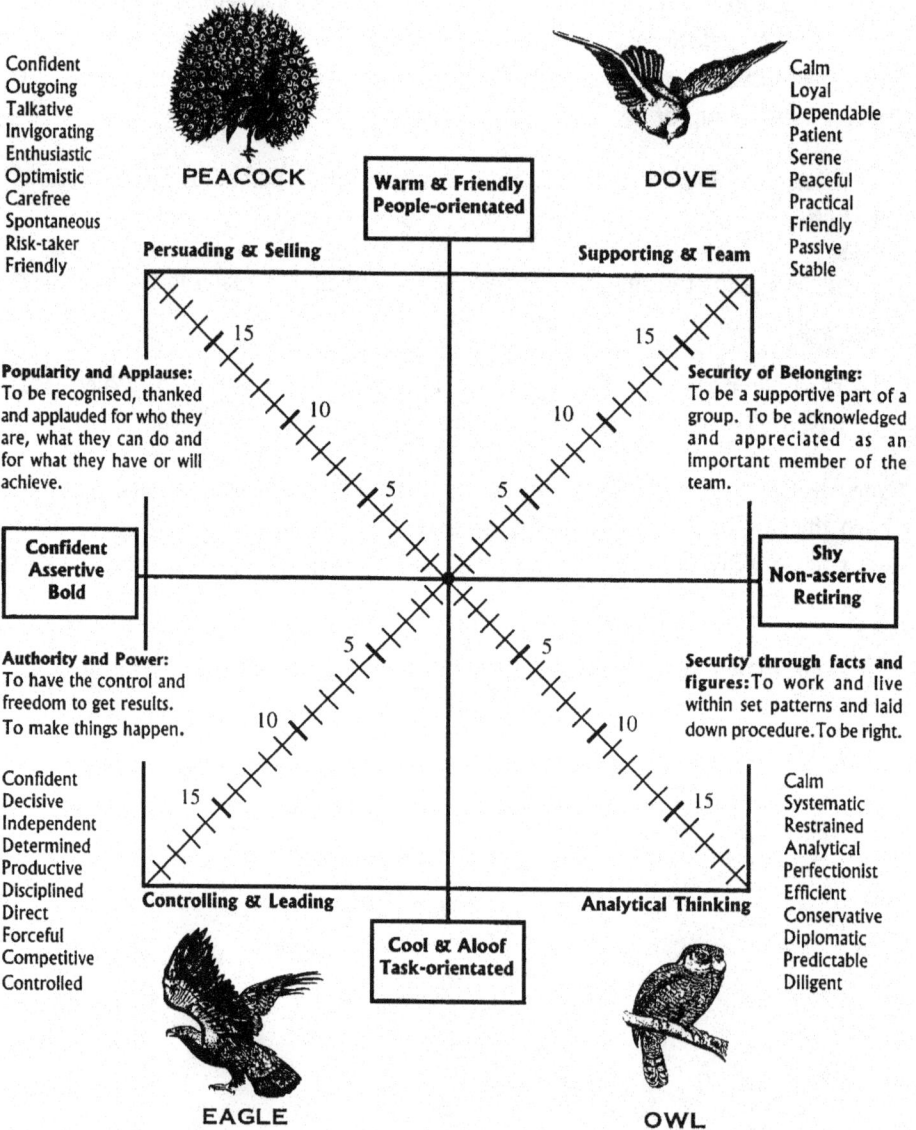

Confident
Outgoing
Talkative
Invigorating
Enthusiastic
Optimistic
Carefree
Spontaneous
Risk-taker
Friendly

PEACOCK

Warm & Friendly
People-orientated

DOVE

Calm
Loyal
Dependable
Patient
Serene
Peaceful
Practical
Friendly
Passive
Stable

Persuading & Selling

Supporting & Team

Popularity and Applause:
To be recognised, thanked and applauded for who they are, what they can do and for what they have or will achieve.

15

10

5

15

10

5

Security of Belonging:
To be a supportive part of a group. To be acknowledged and appreciated as an important member of the team.

Confident
Assertive
Bold

Shy
Non-assertive
Retiring

Authority and Power:
To have the control and freedom to get results.
To make things happen.

5

10

15

5

10

15

Security through facts and figures: To work and live within set patterns and laid down procedure. To be right.

Confident
Decisive
Independent
Determined
Productive
Disciplined
Direct
Forceful
Competitive
Controlled

Controlling & Leading

Cool & Aloof
Task-orientated

Analytical Thinking

Calm
Systematic
Restrained
Analytical
Perfectionist
Efficient
Conservative
Diplomatic
Predictable
Diligent

EAGLE

OWL

SCORING THE QUESTIONNAIRE

The highest score indicates your most dominant style. The next highest score is your secondary style.

Only consider scores above 10 to ascertain your preferred styles.

Take the highest score as the first, and the next highest score as the second.

For example, if you scored Peacock 8, Dove 14, Owl 11, Eagle 7, you would be described as a Dove/Owl.

HIGHS AND LOWS

Anything 7 or below is considered as being low in that particular style. Anything between 8 and 10 is considered as average. Any score between 11 and 14 is above average. 15 to 16 is high. And 17 to 20 is considered extreme.

> 0-7   LOW
> 8-10   AVERAGE
> 11-14   ABOVE AVERAGE
> 15-16   HIGH
> 17-24   EXTREME

OVER 12 IN THREE SCORES

If you have scored over 12 in three or more scores, it may be worth having another look at the questions and your answers to them. Perhaps you are at a stage in your life where you are trying to be 'all things to all people'. If this is the case, it may be causing you frustration and discomfort because you are finding it hard to be 'just you'. It could be time to re-assess your goals and directions.

EXTREME SCORES

If you have scored 17 to 24 in any of the categories, and your graph appears like an arrowhead, similar to the two examples shown on page 74 and 75, then you should refer to the 'Extreme' profile descriptions.

It may pay you to also consider how well you are presently equipped to deal with those people who do not share the same view of life as you. This dominance in your particular style may be seen by others as inflexibility.

Refer to the section 'To Be More Effective' in your particular description. This can give you a guide to the strategies you may need to think about to become more effective with those around you.

FLEXIBILITY

Flexibility gives us the opportunity to move into another's world. It helps us to see life as they see it. It helps to give us empathy. Empathy is the ability to walk in another's shoes. But you have to take your own off first! Empathy and understanding are the keys to unlocking the secrets of 'The People Business'.

LIMITATIONS

Keep in mind that we are all unique. None of us fit neatly and exactly into boxes.

The following profile descriptions are meant to help us understand the differences between each other, our preferences for the way we think, feel and act, our natural specialisations.

As with any questionnaire and descriptions of human nature, this one has its limitations. At best they are about 80 per cent accurate for about 80 per cent of the population. This one is no different. After reading your profile description, if you feel that around 80 per cent is fairly accurate then this is probably the window of life you feel most comfortable looking out of. If not, you may like to have another look at how accurately you answered the questions, or get somebody else to answer them for you.

EXAMPLES OF SCORES

DOVE/OWL

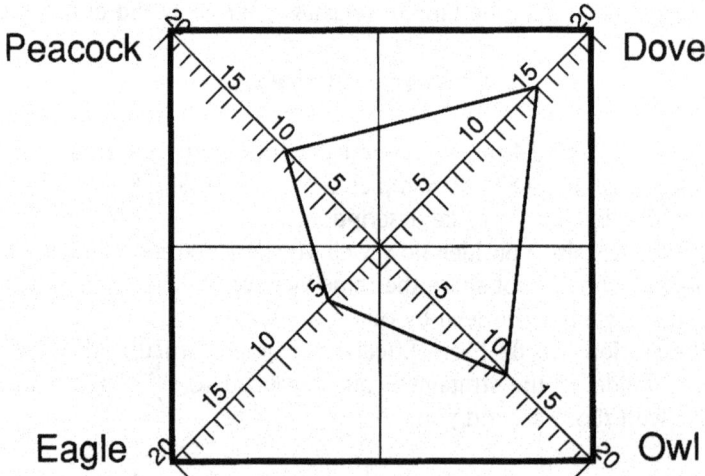

PEACOCK/EAGLE

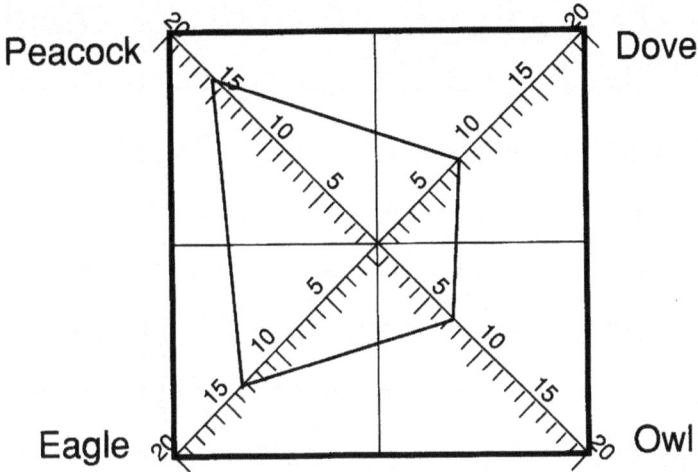

EAGLE/OWL

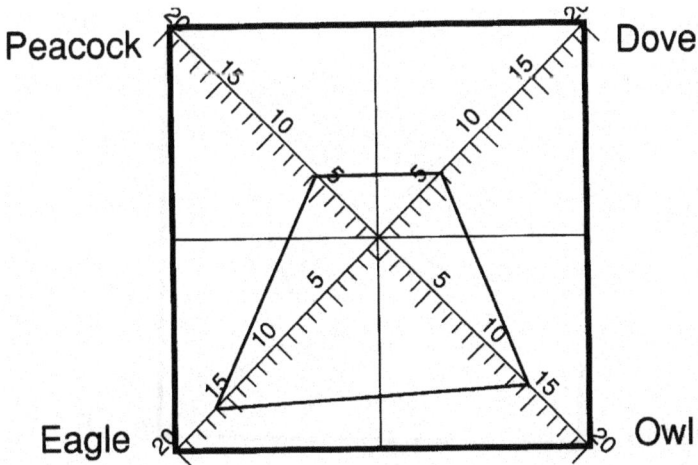

PEACOCK/DOVE

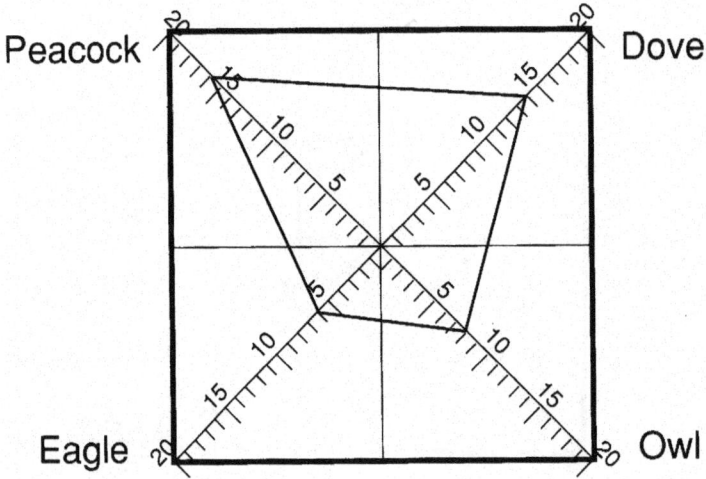

EXTREME DOVE

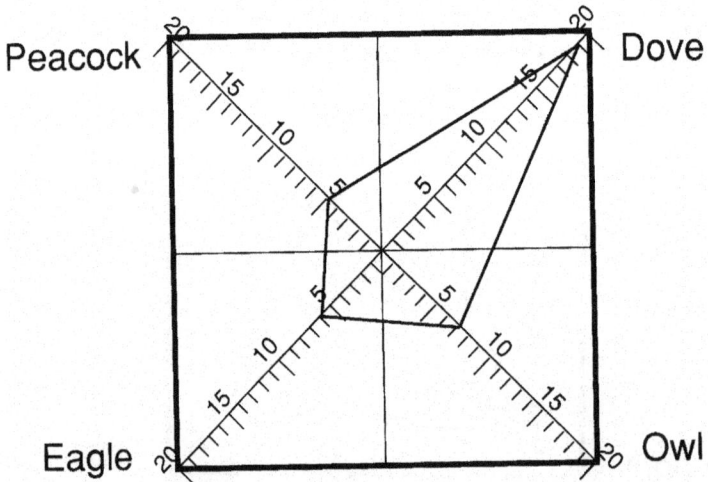

EXTREME EAGLE

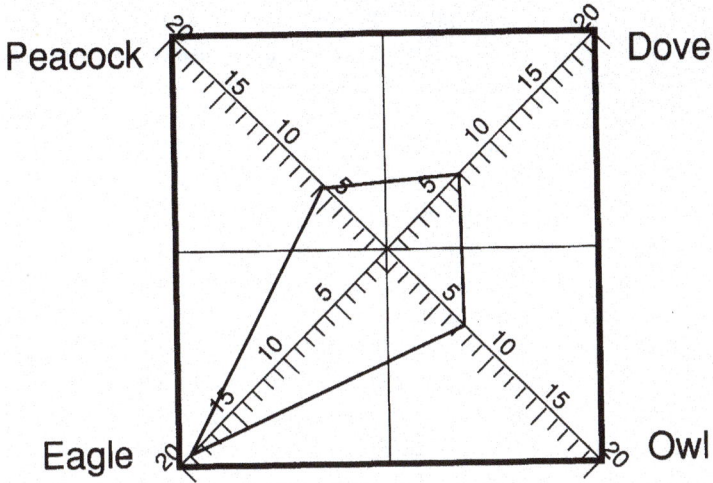

See the next section for a full
description of each of the 16
personality styles.

EXTREME PEACOCK

The Extreme Peacock is confident, talkative, friendly and optimistic. They like to be popular and in the spotlight. They are quick and spontaneous in actions and decisions, sometimes dramatically so. They find sustained listening without the chance to talk uncomfortable and tiring. They are generally enthusiastic, excitable and optimistic.

They tend to jump from one activity to another. They are good starters but poor finishers. They can get others excited and caught up in their dreams and ideas through their naturally strong verbal persuasive skills. They like to be where the action is. They are ambitious and achievement orientated.

They are great name-droppers and storytellers. They will let you know how important they are, and how many important friends they have.

Their body language is fast and very expressive. Lots of facial expressions and sweeping hand gestures accompany their strong verbal persuasive skills. They use strong glowing language that excites and stimulates. They are always on the move.

They like "nice things". Appearances are very important. They are concerned with how others see them. Their dress is normally stylish and fashionable and can be quite flamboyant and showy, especially when it comes to jewellery. They like bold dominant colours both on them and around their environment.

Because recognition and status symbols are important to them, they will go into debt to "look good". Their clothes, jewellery, car, house and office are an expression of themselves and their achievements, both real and imagined. Their work desk normally looks as if a hurricane has just been through their office. But they will tidy-up and look good if they know somebody important is coming.

WANTS Recognition, approval, applause and popularity for who they are and what they can do. Wants to be noticed and in the spotlight. Thrives on status symbols and the admiration of others. They want to be famous!

ADMIRES Achievers and quick thinkers with good verbal skills.

INFLUENCES They influence others with their enthusiasm, optimism, confidence, friendliness and verbal skills.

STRENGTHS Enthusiastic and optimistic. Ability to motivate others. Good verbal and persuasive skills. Able to think in broad concepts. Ideas generator. Invigorating and animated. Likes people. Able to work quickly and excitingly with others. A risk taker. Will take on new and challenging projects.

SHORTCOMINGS They are undisciplined when it comes to time. They dislike being alone and out of the spotlight. Dislikes detailed analytical work and paperwork in general. Exaggerates and generalises when relating 'facts'. They never let the facts mess up a good story. Jumps from one activity to another. Poor finisher. Disorganised. Their natural enthusiasm will often make them take on more than they can handle. They tend to promise more than they can deliver. They are excitable, impatient and manipulative when their own ends are not being met.

UNDER PRESSURE Under pressure the Extreme Peacock will fly off the handle with lots of emotion, noise and drama. They are volatile and loud. They will personalise their attacks using strong emotional language. But once they have got it off their chest, they will usually quickly seek the favour and acceptance of the target of their attack. Peacocks fight first and become friendly after.

FEARS Being taken advantage of. Being 'conned'. Being locked into routine and boring tasks where there is little opportunity for contact with people or the chance to display their talents. They fear being ignored or overlooked.

TO BE MORE EFFECTIVE If you are an Extreme Peacock you could be more effective with more self-discipline, especially time and task disciplines. Try creating tighter goals, objectives, and time frames to keep you on track. Don't promise so much. Be realistic. Try being more analytical. Weigh up the pros and cons more before jumping in feet first. Also, try listening more and talking less. Give it a try. You may find it will help you achieve recognition of your natural talents a lot quicker.

PEACOCK-DOVE

The Peacock-Dove is warm, witty and good fun to be with. They have a keen interest in other people. They are easygoing, very approachable, friendly and understanding. They are sympathetic and tactful with a willing ear for other people's problems. Because of this, they make excellent counsellors, helpers, and customer service people, in fact any job that requires dealing with people. They are people-people.

They are very sensitive to other people's feelings. They do not impose or force their ideas or suggestions on others, even though they themselves have strongly held beliefs about what they believe to be right and wrong, especially about life styles.

Because they are sensitive, and care about other people's feelings, they can often be overly patient and tolerant of others. They do not like making demands on people, or telling others what to do. Because of this, they often appear 'too soft' when it comes to being responsible for getting other people to do what sometimes 'must' be done, whether they like it, or not.

Because of their sensitivity, they can often take criticism of their work as a personal attack and can be offended easily. On the other hand, they respond warmly to praise for a job well done.

Peacock-Doves are optimistic, witty, active, trusting and understanding. They are people-people who make loyal and lovable friends. Socially friendly and charming, their natural talents often find them into the P.R. or helping professions.

WANTS To be with people. To maintain friendly relationships, and pleasant atmospheres, where people are happy.

ADMIRES People who look for, and see, the good in other people.

INFLUENCES They influence others through their warmth and caring attitude.

STRENGTHS Caring, friendly, loyal, and dependable.

SHORTCOMINGS Tends to over-use tolerance, patience and indirectness when dealing with others who are less willing or more assertive than themselves. Does not want to upset anyone.

UNDER PRESSURE Avoids confrontation and conflict. Becomes pliant and persuadable to others' wishes.

FEARS Taking advantage of people. And being taken for granted.

TO BE MORE EFFECTIVE If you are a Peacock-Dove you could be more effective with less concern about how others feel about you. You can't please all the people all the time, so why try so hard? Not everybody is going to love you! Perhaps try paying more attention to your own needs and less on other people's. You might also look at setting tighter time deadlines to do things, or stop promising so much. Give it some thought. It might be a step in the right direction.

PEACOCK-EAGLE

Optimistic, energetic, friendly and enthusiastic, the Peacock-Eagle has the natural ability to gain the respect and confidence of all types of people.

They are confident, warm, friendly, trusting and impulsive. They inspire enthusiasm in others and spread goodwill.

Sometimes they can be too trusting and optimistic, especially about their ability to motivate those who do not want to be motivated.

They are initiators and innovators of new ideas who work in high spurts of energy and activity.

When they are up they are really up, but when they are down they are really down. There is no in between for the Peacock-Eagle.

They are imaginative, good talkers and persuaders, and good starters (but not always good finishers) who work well with other people, especially in a leadership role.

They are actively dominant and confident, and because of this, they tend to win positions of authority, prestige and status which is an important driving force to them. They love a challenge and the recognition and rewards that go with accomplishment.

They are witty, good humoured, socially charming and generally take people as they find them.

They hate being locked into structure and routine. Rather, they thrive on change, challenge and fast moving situations. You could describe them as 'Adventurers'. Yet they are also logical, objective and organised.

They are extremely good at promoting themselves, their ideas or anything else they believe in. Their natural talents often lead them into leadership positions, selling, acting and politics.

WANTS   To achieve results which in turn will give them the recognition and applause that go with those results and achievement. Wants recognition and status.

ADMIRES   Achievement. And the ability to verbalise and articulate ideas and concepts in a persuasive way.

INFLUENCES   Peacock-Eagles influence others through their warmth, charm and persuasive manner.

STRENGTHS   Enthusiasm, optimism, warmth and persuasive abilities.

SHORTCOMINGS They tend to become restless, fidgety and impatient when not challenged or in the spotlight. Can tend to overuse optimism and enthusiasm and come on too strong at times.

UNDER PRESSURE Becomes emotional and dramatic, then becomes compliant.

FEARS Being locked into a routine. No challenge. No adventure. No opportunity to use imagination and persuasive skills. Not being recognised for their talents.

TO BE MORE EFFECTIVE If you are a Peacock-Eagle you could increase your effectiveness by listening more, and talking less. Ask more questions, rather than making statements. Use more patience when dealing with those who are not as fast as you. Slow down a bit. It might be a step in the right direction. Give it a try.

PEACOCK-OWL

The Peacock/Owl is confident, outgoing, friendly and self-assured. They are socially poised, witty and charming with a natural ability to involve and harness those around them into helping them achieve their goals.

They are optimistic and calculated risk takers. They take creative ideas and concepts and give them practical applications. They are creative as well as logical and practical, and possess a high drive factor to win at whatever they take on. They like to strive for, and get, results.

The Peacock-Owl is a good talker and persuader with the ability to win others to their point of view, using facts and logic rather than emotions. Slower people can often feel over-powered by their force of logical persuasion and enthusiasm.

Getting the job done in the easiest and most practical way, as well as being popular with those around them is important to the Peacock-Owl. They like social approval as well as being recognised for their skills and abilities. Because of this, leadership roles, and the accompanying prestige and recognition that goes with it is important to them.

They like a challenge and a fast pace. They tend to work in spurts of high energy. Many find it difficult to keep up with them. When this happens, the Peacock-Owl can tend to lack tolerance and become impatient and critical.

They become restless quickly and lose interest in situations that lack competition and challenge. They like to be where the action is. The Peacock-Owl likes to organise the parade, and then lead it. And once the parade is over, they will look for another one.

They are self-starters, fast paced, competitive, witty and fun to be involved with, while at the same time they are logical and analytical in their search for the most direct way of achieving results. Their natural talents lead them into leadership and management roles.

WANTS To initiate action, lead the team, and achieve results, while at the same time remain popular with the people around them.

ADMIRES People who initiate action. People that get things done.

INFLUENCES Peacock-Owls influence others through their persuasive skills, their fast pace and their competitiveness.

STRENGTHS Enthusiasm, persuasiveness and practical approach. Getting things done through people while maintaining a harmonious atmosphere.

SHORTCOMINGS They can tend to overuse their authority and natural assertiveness. They can become fidgety and impatient with slower people. They can come on too strong at times.

UNDER PRESSURE Becomes restless, impatient and critical using logic and reason.

FEARS Not being able to get results. Not being influential. Not winning.

TO BE MORE EFFECTIVE If you are a Peacock-Owl, try to relax a little more, be less intense, particularly with people who do not always measure up to your high expectations. Slowing down and using a little more tolerance and patience might be a step in the right direction. It is worth a try.

EXTREME DOVE

The Extreme Dove is warm, friendly and shy with strangers.

They are extremely caring, supportive and people-orientated. They share their personal feelings and have a willing ear for others' problems. They are good friends and team members who are reliable and loyal. Pleasant and friendly, they tend to like to stay in the same place, whether it be a home, or a job. They avoid risk and do not like change or disruptions to their normal pattern of doing things.

They are good listeners with empathetic counselling skills. They are good at performing tasks in an accepted pattern.

Patient and tolerant, placid and peaceful, they make warm and loyal friends, co-workers and partners. They like the company of other people and find a sense of security in dealing with people and situations they are familiar with.

Slower paced and relaxed, they are intent listeners with good eye contact, attentive smiles and nods. They show interest through their facial expressions. They are warm, friendly and non-threatening.

Plants, flowers and photographs of their family and friends will be found about them. At work they may well have Band-Aids, biscuits or sweets in their desk drawer 'In case somebody should need them'. Their environment is people orientated, warm and welcoming; 'homely'. They prefer to sit on the same side of the desk with you. A poster with the theme of 'Caring' may well hang on their office wall. They like to create a 'people-are-important' atmosphere whether at home or at work.

WANTS To help people. And wants the security of dealing with non-threatening people and familiar situations.

ADMIRES People who look for the good in other people. Friendship and loyalty. Evenness of mood and temperament.

INFLUENCES They influence others through their warmth, dependability and loyalty.

STRENGTHS Friendly and supportive. A reliable team player. Good at performing jobs in accepted patterns and routines. Good at concentrating on repetitive tasks. Patience, tolerance, loyalty. Good with people.

SHORTCOMINGS Extreme Doves are not good at working in unpredictable environments, nor reacting quickly to change. They are also not good at doing many things at once, or telling people what to do. They shy away from risk.

UNDER PRESSURE When the Extreme Dove is threatened or put under pressure they withdraw into themselves and away from the person or situation which is causing the discomfort. They become submissive. Under attack the Dove takes flight.

FEARS Being pushed into the spotlight. Telling people what to do. Working or living in unpredictable environments. Changes to their normal way of doing things. Dealing with difficult people.

TO BE MORE EFFECTIVE To be more effective, the Extreme Dove needs to develop a little more confidence and assertiveness. They need to gain a stronger belief in who they are and what they can do. They need to ask people less and assert their own opinion more. They need to say 'no' more often for their own sake. They need to speed up a bit and take a few more risks. They need to spend less time relating to people who do not want it and who perhaps do not deserve their natural warmth, loyalty and sincerity.

DOVE-PEACOCK

The Dove-Peacock is patient, controlled, moderate and reflective. They move with care, deliberation and moderation in most of the things they do.

They prefer to take a low profile in most situations, particularly with assertive people, yet can be fiercely independent and stubborn when something they believe in is threatened.

They generally appear passive, unruffled and unconcerned, even under stress, but inside there is a storm going on.

They approach most situations with care and concentration and are conscious of how those around them feel. They are constantly tuned in to other people's feelings. They are supportive of others and make ideal team members. They make people feel both wanted and needed.

Dove-Peacocks are adaptable, steady workers who prefer, and can be relied upon, to carry out their work in an accepted and approved pattern. They would also prefer to be part of the team rather than being the leader and having to make the hard decisions. Never the less, they can be quite independent and self sufficient when it comes to getting a job done.

They are steady, reserved, conservative and conventional, and can sometimes appear shy and restrained. But they have a fierce and loyal commitment to the people and organisations which are important to them.

They make kind, warm, devoted and protective parents and friends. They strive to maintain happy relationships. These natural talents often find them working in nursing, counselling, social work and the other 'helping' professions.

WANTS To be accepted by others. To be an important part of a family, group or team. They want to contribute.

ADMIRES People who are steady, loyal and dependable.

INFLUENCES They influence others through their warmth, kindness, friendship and loyalty.

STRENGTHS Caring, friendly, predictable, trusting, supportive. Being of service to people.

SHORTCOMINGS Can tend to be too kind and trusting sometimes, particularly with those who can tend to take advantage of their good nature.

UNDER PRESSURE   Becomes adaptable and compliant. Says 'yes' but really means 'no'.

FEARS   Aggressive people and conflict situations.

TO BE MORE EFFECTIVE   If you are a Dove-Peacock, you could become more effective by gaining a little more assertiveness and firmness in saying 'no' to others more often. Some people tend to take advantage of your good nature. Give 'no' a try. It may be a small step in the right direction to doing the things you want to do rather than doing what others want you to do. Give it a try and see what happens.

DOVE-EAGLE

The Dove-Eagle comprises a very small percentage of the population. Their talents are extremely rare.

They are deep, creative thinkers, and others find them very hard to understand at times. They often display an image of aloofness and detachment, but they are far from detached. Pre-occupied with their thoughts would be a better description.

They are curious and idealistic with strong powers of analytical reasoning and the use of logic in seeking out facts and ideas.

They are steady, reliable and unassuming. Patience and steadiness are their strong virtues. Because of this, they are consistent and conservative, and do not like changes in their home or work environment. They like things to stay the way they are.

They are generally shy and withdrawn in a social situation, preferring relationships which are familiar and which have been built up over a long time. They make strong and loyal friends and partners. But do not expect too many parties or new social situations to be on their agenda.

Because of their natural skills in being good at working on complex and involved problems, they are often attracted to the teaching or intellectual pursuits, science and research, and areas where they can take on one thing at a time and not be rushed. In other words, they take on jobs requiring high degrees of specialisation in an environment where tight dead-lines are not as important as the correctness of the ideas and the facts involved.

WANTS To have a predictable and systematic home and work environment free of risk, change, or disruption.

ADMIRES People who have patience and steadiness. Objective thinking, intelligence and competence.

INFLUENCES They influence others through their consistency of mood and behaviour, and their knowledge and skills in a specialised area.

STRENGTHS Objective and reasoned thinking. Consistent and even tempered. Highly specialised skills.

SHORTCOMINGS Tends to overuse patience, conservatism and the avoidance of taking risks.

UNDER PRESSURE Withdraws, complies with other's wishes.

FEARS Changing environments. Risks.

TO BE MORE EFFECTIVE If you are a Dove-Eagle you could become more effective by taking more risks in the people-relations area, particularly with people who are more assertive than you. Try being a little less self-conscious and be more open with others. Let people inside your world. Give it a try. It might be a step in the right direction.

DOVE-OWL

The Dove-Owl is conservative, shy, dependable and modest. They do everything in moderation.

They are quiet and sensitive people who are concerned with maintaining set patterns of doing things, and avoiding anything that may appear rushed or risky. They like to keep themselves to themselves and work in familiar and low-risk environments.

They are patient and deliberate in what they do, and do not like to be rushed. They like to be in possession of all the facts, the more the better, before making a decision. And even when they do have all the information, they tend to avoid making decisions. They always want to be 'correct' and yet are at odds to know what 'correct' is.

Their natural skills make them specialists in whatever interests them. They are good with both their head and their hands. They are accurate, logical and precise, and can be very artistic and creative. They can become quite absorbed in something to the exclusion of everything else.

They are loyal and intense to causes they care about. They are moderate and modest in their dealings with other people, and build close relationships with only a small group of trusted friends. To these people, they are trusting, open and generous.

They are good at organising ideas and facts rather than organising people. They are steady-paced and persistent performers who are slow to adapt to change. They feel more comfortable and secure with laid down procedures, structures and habits of doing things. Because of this, they can tend to ignore or overlook quicker or more efficient ways of getting things done.

Because of their special talents, they can often tend to 'bury' themselves in a narrow field of interest, and become totally absorbed to the exclusion of anything else. Some of our artists and sculptors throughout history have been Dove-Owls.

WANTS   To apply their skills and talents in a non-changing and predictable environment where they will not be rushed for results.

ADMIRES   People who are loyal and committed. Competency and consistency. Trustworthiness.

INFLUENCES   They influence others through their steadiness, consistency, and specialised skills in a given field.

STRENGTHS   They maintain harmony and consistency. Reliable, trustworthy, loyal, patient and dependable. Self-disciplined.

SHORTCOMINGS Tends to over-use habits and set procedures. Can be over-conservative. Avoids change. Over-avoids risks.

UNDER PRESSURE Tends to become withdrawn. Becomes over-compliant and over-adaptable to authority. Goes along with others' wishes but seethes inside. Can become silently stubborn and unmovable.

FEARS Aggression and conflict situations. Change. Not being given enough time to get organised. Unpredictable situations. Too little time to think things through. Pressure.

TO BE MORE EFFECTIVE If you are a Dove-Owl you could become more effective by taking the occasional risk. Try jumping in feet first now and again, rather than pondering on a situation for so long. Be a little more assertive, especially when you feel you are right. Speak up for yourself more. Stop worrying so much about what other people think. Give it a go. It might be a step in the right direction.

EXTREME EAGLE

The Extreme Eagle is controlled, cool, dominant, and self-assured.

They do not like listening, especially to excuses.

They are fast paced, assertive and definitely in control of themselves and those around them. They like to be the boss in any situation. They tell people what to do.

Decisive in actions and decisions, they hate inaction and not being in control of things.

Cool, independent and highly competitive, they get short and impatient with non-performers. They also have a very low tolerance for any display of feelings or emotions expressed by others.

They prefer maximum freedom to manage themselves and others. Because of their abruptness, they can be seen as autocratic, dominant and over-bearing when those around them are not living up to their expectations.

They will often put work before pleasure. Achievement and results, getting the job done, is everything to the Extreme Eagle. They love a challenge. They are the workaholics of life.

Their body language is fast and efficient. Expressions are generally cool and controlled. Little emotion is shown. They can be abrupt and seemingly oblivious of the little 'people things' that are happening around them.

Those that work for them often perceive them as undiplomatic, critical and bossy. They have little patience for 'small talk'. 'My way or the highway' is a constant theme when it comes to how things should be done.

They are generally unconcerned with style and fashion. Dress is efficient and practical, as are their surroundings. Rather than pictures, they will usually have a planner and graphs on the walls of their office. Anything that does not help in getting results, such as paintings, decor, furnishings and stylish clothing is considered superfluous. Clothes are normally of sober and conservative colours.

WANTS   Achievement. Results. Challenge. Positions of power and authority. Wants to be the boss.

ADMIRES   People who get results. Fast!

INFLUENCES   They influence others through their directness and ability to independently get what they set out to get.

STRENGTHS   Getting results and causing action. Accepting a challenge. Making decisions. Getting things done. Taking autocratic leadership roles. Highly self-disciplined. Good at bringing about change.

SHORTCOMINGS Tends to question authority and work outside of the rules, but will make sure others work within them. Not comfortable at being 'just part of the team', wants to be the boss. Not good at using caution or calculating the risks. At times can go to uneconomical and extreme lengths to achieve their goals. Can be disruptive and cause trouble when no challenge or scope is in the job. Low tolerance with 'slower people'. Does not like listening, especially to explanations or excuses. They can be very domineering and intimidating to those around them.

UNDER PRESSURE If things are not going the way the Extreme Eagle wants them to go, they can become domineering and bossy using facts, or logic, or sarcasm, or all three wrapped up in one venomous onslaught. And if things do not get better, the Extreme Eagle will turn off, avoid or ignore either the stressful situation, or the person causing it. The Extreme Eagle is a fighter, then a flighter. When the Eagle loses interest THAT IS IT!

FEARS Not being influential. Not being in control. Not being the boss. Being bored and unchallenged.

TO BE MORE EFFECTIVE To be more effective the Extreme Eagle needs to take life a little less seriously, to slow down and relax more. They need to acquire more patience and tolerance when dealing with those who are not as fast paced as they are. They need to not be so rigid and unbending. They need to try dropping back a gear or two and take a little more time to relate to people more. They need to try asking more instead of telling, especially asking other peoples opinions, otherwise they run the risk of appearing insensitive, uncaring and impatient. They also need to weigh up the pros and cons a little more before rushing into decisions, particularly in regard to the effect their quick decisions can have on the people around them, and their feelings.

EAGLE-PEACOCK

The Eagle-Peacock is assertive, confident, enthusiastic and adventurous. They can be seen by some as warm and charming, and by others as having confidence verging on arrogance.

They get results in just about everything they get involved with. They work in high spurts of creative energy. Challenge, accomplishment and achievement is everything to the Eagle-Peacock.

Forceful, friendly, diplomatic and socially adept, they think and move with a fast-preoccupied purpose and direction. They do not like being told what to do, but are good at telling others what to do.

They can be quite independent yet still be extremely popular. They are natural generators of creative ideas with the skills to adapt those ideas into practical ways that will achieve their goals and objectives.

They can be quite impatient and critical of slower moving people, and quite demanding when things are not going their way. Yet at the same time they can be warm, sociable, sympathetic and generous to those they feel deserve their attention.

Imaginative, optimistic and highly competitive with good verbal and persuasive skills, the Eagle-Peacocks' natural talents and abilities often lead them into positions of leadership and politics.

They can be both charming and intimidating. They are individualists who hate to be seen as 'soft', and fear being manipulated in any way, yet at the same time they are quite capable of manipulating others to get what they want.

Eagle-Peacocks are forceful, daring and decisive risk-takers who thrive on challenge and achievement. Many of the leaders and politicians through-out history have been Eagle-Peacocks.

WANTS Challenge and the creative freedom to achieve results. The power and the authority to bring about change. Wants to make things happen.

ADMIRES People who can get things done quickly. Achievers and adventurers.

INFLUENCES They influence others through their self-motivation, persistence, self- discipline and force of character. Their ability to get things done.

STRENGTHS Goal orientated. The ability to bring about change and get results whilst still remaining popular.

SHORTCOMINGS Tends to over-use 'I know best' attitude. Can become over-forceful and impatient when things are not going their way.

UNDER PRESSURE Tends to become short-tempered, bossy and critical. Lets others know how they are feeling in no uncertain terms.

FEARS Not being taken seriously enough. Being taken advantage of. Being used. Being too soft. Not having the freedom and authority to get results.

TO BE MORE EFFECTIVE If you are an Eagle-Peacock you could be more effective with patience, tolerance and flexibility when dealing with slower people. Perhaps a few more explanations to those around you for the reasons behind your decisions could also help. You must remember you have the speed of a Maserati. Come back to second gear now and again and let the others catch up with you. It is worth a try.

EAGLE-DOVE

The Eagle-Dove is energetic, loyal, friendly and tactful, with a deep sense of duty towards their goals and the people and organisations they care about.

They are conscientious, diligent and have a high opinion of their personal ability and worth. They have strong commitments to their personal goals and to traditional values. They will not stay in situations or environments where their personal goals, or values, are being frustrated or compromised.

They are initiators and achievers with a definite sense of mission and direction. They are versatile and optimistic and immerse themselves 'boots and all' in jobs and interests that challenge them. They are rarely idle or at loose ends looking for something to do.

They find it hard to delegate important tasks to others because they are concerned that it will not be done as well as they could do it themselves.

Whether they win or lose, they are prepared to take either the applause or the blame. The song, 'I Did It My Way' was written for the Eagle-Dove.

They are individualists who have a strong inner drive to achieve that is coupled with a definite sense of right and wrong. They find it extremely difficult to compromise their personal goals and sense of values, both of which are high.

They are practical and realistic people who strive for harmony and the maintaining of established structures and systems. Yet they are individualists and self-reliant doers.

If you want a job done that needs to get concrete results, and the Eagle-Dove is interested in the challenge, and agrees with your values, then this is the person to get. But be prepared to meet their high standards.

WANTS To achieve meaningful personal and challenging goals.

ADMIRES People who get results whilst still maintaining their integrity.

INFLUENCES They influence others through their initiative and the ability to get results on time, on their own.

STRENGTHS High personal standards. Self-reliance. The ability to get things done.

SHORTCOMINGS Tends to become over-engrossed in tasks to the exclusion of almost everything else. Tends to over-use self-reliance. Not needing others.

UNDER PRESSURE Tends to become short, impatient and blunt with others. Becomes critical. Over-uses 'If you want a job done properly, then do it yourself'.

FEARS That the people they are involved with may have lesser standards or values than they do. Not getting results.

TO BE MORE EFFECTIVE If you are an Eagle-Dove you could become more effective with a little more flexibility to compromise. Have more trust in other people's ability, or their potential ability. Give those around you the chance to have a go and make a few mistakes because that is how we all learn and grow. And don't be such a perfectionist. Give it some thought. It might be worth a try.

EAGLE-OWL

The Eagle-Owl projects an outward image of being logical, realistic, cool and blunt. Small talk, diplomacy and socialising are not the Eagle-Owl's preferred activities, although they can be quite outgoing and charming when they want to be.

They are organised, systematic and objective. On the one hand they are logical and analytical, and on the other, they are interested in the unusual and creative. They are excellent problem solvers.

Mixed within them is a highly geared resolve for accomplishment and results plus an equal desire for perfection. Generally these two forces result in the Eagle-Owl achieving the balance of getting it done right without taking too long.

They are accurate and deliberate. They tend to be quick to make the daily decisions, yet they can be extreme procrastinators when it comes to the big decisions.

They seek out the facts and details, and all the angles. The freedom and authority to get results is important to them. They are pragmatists.

Facts transcend feelings as far as the Eagle-Owl is concerned. Results and practicality, rather than social poise and small talk makes them often appear cool and calculating. They are hard to get close to.

They have definite and unbending opinions of 'right' and 'wrong' in their personal standards and life in general. It has been said that there is only 'their way' and the 'wrong way' by those who know them well. At work they tend to be respected rather than popular. They can be chronic workaholics.

Their natural talents often find them in controlling positions. Many military leaders throughout history have been Eagle-Owls.

WANTS Unusual and creative challenges. To be influential in bringing about action and results. The authority and power to get the job done.

ADMIRES People with the ability to get things done on time, and done right the first time. People with high personal standards of efficiency.

INFLUENCES They influence others through their 'no nonsense' attitude, rapid daily decision making, and problem solving skills. Getting things done.

STRENGTHS Assertive, controlled and pioneering. A systematic initiator in bringing about either change or bottom line results. Self-motivated and disciplined.

SHORTCOMINGS Puts tasks before people. Tends to over-use criticism and bluntness. Lacks everyday diplomacy and tolerance for the foibles of human nature.

UNDER PRESSURE Becomes cool, critical and assertive using logic and reason rather than emotions. Can become sulky.

FEARS Being bored and unchallenged. Not being in a position to influence what is, or could be, happening.

TO BE MORE EFFECTIVE If you are an Eagle-Owl perhaps you could be more effective by slowing down and relating more to those who are not as fast and logical as you are. Use tact and diplomacy more, some small talk of a personal nature. Loosen up a bit. Humans are not always 'correct', that is what makes us human. Life is too short to be that serious about everything! Give it some thought. It might be worth a try in the long run.

EXTREME OWL

The Extreme Owl is thoughtful and introspective and can appear shy, cool and distant.

Quiet and analytical, they are slower-paced and show little, if any, outward feelings or emotions. They are hard to get to know.

In the Extreme Owl's world there is a place for everything and everything is in its place.

Independent and individualistic, they prefer to work alone. They like their privacy and solitude.

Cautious and extremely conservative, they are definitely not risk takers.

Extreme Owls are always looking for statistics, evidence facts and proof. Suspicious and sceptical, they are always looking for 'the catch'. They want to see the guarantees. They tend to buy only the tried and proven, the safest.

They have great respect for rules and accepted procedures, law and order.

They dislike social situations. They prefer doing tasks rather than having to deal with people.

They are systematic, analytical, persistent, serious and exacting. They will often use the saying, 'Fools rush in where wise men fear to tread', as a justification for indecision and inaction.

Their body language is almost wooden. There is little or no animation and lacks spontaneity. Eye contact is infrequent. There is little emotion or facial expression.

They tend to wear conservative and sober colours, especially brown and autumn colours. There is little preoccupation with clothes, fashion or style. Little sense of 'what goes with what'.

Their work place is usually sterile and efficient. They generally have planners and graphs on the wall and manuals and reference texts in their bookshelves.

WANTS Security through set procedures, facts, data, law and order. No risk. No change.

ADMIRES Conservatism and correctness.

INFLUENCES They influence others through their ability to be dependably accurate and precise.

STRENGTHS Diligent, accurate, systematic, persistent, organised, precise. Upholder of rules and set procedures. Objective and analytical. Cautious in actions and decisions. Good problem solving and critical thinking skills. Self-disciplined. Good at following directives.

SHORTCOMINGS Stiff, picky, righteous and pessimistic. Over reliance on rules and procedures, data and information collection. Low risk taker. Slow at making decisions. Slow to delegate.

UNDER PRESSURE Under pressure, particularly when forced to make a quick decision, the Owl will avoid. When under stress, the Owl takes flight. Becomes worried and fussy.

FEARS Unpredictability. The unexpected. Acting without hard statistical data or proven facts, or a proven system.

TO BE MORE EFFECTIVE To be more effective the Extreme Owl needs to be less critical, moralistic and stuffy. Less picky and detail orientated. They need to be a little more flexible in their thinking. Accept a few more risks, especially in the people area. They need to try taking the first approach more often rather than analysing a situation to death. They need to speed up their decision making, especially if they want to influence faster moving people. They can be seen by some as a pain in the neck when it comes to detail. They need to try taking a few more risks, especially with people.

OWL-PEACOCK

The Owl-Peacock is rare and only makes up a very small percentage of the population.

They are self-dependent, individualistic, serious, analytical and creative.

They have high personal ambitions and are supremely confident in their ability to match or excel others in personal effort, or use expertise that is familiar to them. They do not crow about this, they are just quietly confident.

They like their solitude and the chance to concentrate in their own space. Their environment is normally well organised and structured.

They have high levels of self-discipline and are usually extremely proficient in a specialised area of expertise and knowledge.

They can be very demanding of themselves and quite self-critical of their own performance if they feel it does not measure up to their own exacting standards.
Owl-Peacocks tend to convey the impression that they know something about everything. They can also tend to convey a rather superior attitude about their way being the 'right way' of doing something.

They have high expectations of themselves and those around them and can become quite critical if these expectations are not met.

The Owl/Peacock hates mistakes. They are creative problem solvers, but tend to want to resolve the problem themselves. They normally do not trust others to get the job done their way, therefore they have trouble delegating the 'important' things. This often results in those around them not being given the chance to develop through making their own mistakes.

They are likeable, devoted and caring people who are sometimes a little hard to get to know. They like things to be harmonious and run smoothly. They are deeply loyal to a small group of trusted friends.

WANTS To achieve their personal goals within a predictable system of harmony and order. Wants to excel in technical proficiency and quality.

ADMIRES Self-discipline, diligence, knowledge and technical proficiency.

INFLUENCES They influence others through their confidence and ability in their given area of expertise. And their reliability and loyalty.

STRENGTHS Excellent specialised skills. Dependable and proficient. Good problem solving skills. Works independently. Good with both technical tasks as well as handling people. Good quality controller.

SHORTCOMINGS Tends to over-assume that others are as proficient and expert as they are and quickly loses faith in them if they're not. Over-uses attitude of superiority. Tend to keep the important jobs to themselves.

UNDER PRESSURE Becomes quiet and restrained, especially sensitive when any hint of criticism is suggested.

FEARS Being too conventional and predictable. Being boring.

TO BE MORE EFFECTIVE If you are an Owl-Peacock, you can become more effective by having more patience with others who are not as naturally gifted as you are. Perhaps you could also try giving a little more appreciation to those around you who are doing the best that they can. Not everybody is as clever as you are in the things you are good at. Try delegating a little more, give others the chance to develop wider skills. Give it some thought. It might be worth a try.

OWL-DOVE

The Owl-Dove is steady, dependable, stable, quiet and modest.

They are supportive, agreeable and tactful. They avoid any hint of risk, conflict or trouble. They like harmony, structure and things to stay the same, both at home and at work. They do not like change. They are our 'solid citizens.'

They are sensitive, kind and sympathetic. They are also conventional and conservative. They like the old fashioned values, and prefer guidelines and policies to be clear and adhered to at work. They like the security of system and order in a fairly sheltered and low risk environment. They tend to stay at the same job well past normal long-service periods.

They are great team people. Loyal, moderate and adaptable, they like to do one thing at a time and do it well, and to do it by the book.

They are quiet, highly sensitive people who can become quite irritable and stubborn when they feel they are being rushed into something. Because of this, they often feel over-worked, 'up-tight' and worried. Tension headaches can be the result. But they tend to suffer in silence.

Owl-Doves are systematic and habit bound. They like to follow set patterns and procedures in both their personal and working lives. They can be seen by some as perfectionists. But this is because they have such a strong and unbending view of the 'right way' and the 'wrong way' of doing things.

Although friendly and sociable, they can be perceived as shy, quiet and withdrawn preferring to listen than do most of the talking. 'Actions speak louder than words' as far as the Owl-Dove is concerned. They are self-conscious and prefer to stay well out of the spotlight. They also tend to be cynical about compliments and look for the 'reasons', or ulterior motives behind why the compliment is being paid.

They are conscientious and hard workers. They are also loyal and devoted friends and partners, sometimes too loyal and devoted, to the point of being martyrs. Joan of Arc may well have been an Owl-Dove. If you ever need a 'friend in need', then you cannot do better than to develop a friendship with an Owl-Dove.

WANTS To belong. And the security of a predictable and unchanging environment with set patterns of doing things and dealing with the same familiar people. Wants harmony and life to be predictable.

ADMIRES People who have high and precise standards and values. And people who are predictable.

INFLUENCES They influence others through their consistency of mood and their steadiness and loyalty.

STRENGTHS Steadfast, systematic, accurate, rational, objective, predictable and loyal. A conformist.

SHORTCOMINGS Tends to over-use the dependency of past habits. Being over-analytical. Holding on too long to familiar structures and systems. Over-cautious when it comes to change.

UNDER PRESSURE Becomes tense and worried, and will over-submit to the demands of others. Adopts an 'Anything for a quiet life' approach to their own detriment.

FEARS Taking risks. Displays of irrational and uncontrolled emotions in others. Antagonism and conflict. Disharmony. Change.

TO BE MORE EFFECTIVE If you are an Owl-Dove you could be more effective by becoming a little more independent and decisive. Be more assertive. Adopt a stronger sense of liking 'who' you are, rather than 'what' you can do. Try becoming your own friend a little more. Risk going outside of your old procedures and habits now and again. Give it a go tomorrow. You never know, it could be a step in the right direction. And it might help those headaches!

OWL-EAGLE

The Owl-Eagle is individualistic, independent, logical, conscientious, determined and efficient.

They are precise, accurate and systematic and hate incompetency in any form, particularly when it is displayed by those around them.

They like order and perfection and are single-minded about achieving them.

They are disciplinarians, both at home and at work. They are 'no nonsense' people.

They can be seen as cool, blunt, stubborn and critical when things are not going the way they want them to go.

Because they like their own privacy and space, they can also be seen by some as aloof and withdrawn

Owl-Eagles do most things in a planned, careful and conservative way, but will modify their position to achieve the goals that are important to them. They are adaptable realists.

Analytical and logical, they tend to question things. They also have strong and definite opinions about their own worth, ability and value.

While generally conservative by nature, they can be quite creative and innovative in putting ideas into practical use, particularly if it helps them achieve their objectives. They also have the ability to be able to make the right decisions at the right time.

Owl-Eagles are systematic and precise thinkers who like structure and order in both their personal and professional lives. They maintain high standards and find delegating responsibility uncomfortable. They tend to keep the important jobs to themselves for fear others will mess them up.

They tend to work in spurts of high energy and concentration. They are confident, competitive and decisive drivers who like to maintain harmony and order.

They are tactful and diplomatic with others, but would generally prefer to work alone in a set and pre-determined manner. Accurate and self-disciplined, they like to keep themselves to themselves.

Their natural talents attract them to jobs where they can put principles and theories into practical solutions. They make efficient engineers, executives and senior public servants.

WANTS Structure and order. Wants people and things to be predictable.

ADMIRES Competency and efficiency in following procedure, orders and directives.

INFLUENCES They influence others through their self-discipline and their ability to plan and achieve results in a structured and pre-determined pattern.

STRENGTHS Self-discipline, diplomacy, decisiveness and determination.

SHORTCOMINGS Puts tasks before people. They tend to over-use rules, procedure and discipline at the expense of human nature. Can tend to keep themselves to themselves a little too much.

UNDER PRESSURE Tends to take the bull by the horns overriding other people's feelings and sense of worth. Becomes cool and critical.

FEARS Lack of structure, procedure and control. Not having a planned and clarified method of approach. Others are being illogical or irrational.

TO BE MORE EFFECTIVE If you are an Owl-Eagle you could be more effective by being less stoic, individualistic and pragmatic. Try for more balance between your concern for getting things done and the people-aspects of the job. Try being a little more open with others. Loosen up a bit. You may even find that the people-side of life can actually be enjoyable. Give it a try. It's worth the risk!

Studies carried out in America on
sudden premature death of people
under 65 showed that the majority
of these people were cynical,
hostile, aggressive and
hated their jobs.

They also discovered that more
people die sudden premature
deaths at 9 am. on Monday
mornings than at
any other time.

SQUARE PEGS IN SQUARE HOLES

Attempting to place people into jobs
they feel comfortable, productive
and happy doing.

NATURAL SKILLS AND COMFORT ZONES

STRESS-RELATED PROBLEMS It has been estimated that up to 85 per cent of our hospital beds are occupied by people with stress-related problems. From ulcers to triple bypasses, and everything in between.

Ulcers aren't caused by what we eat, but by what's eating us.

When we are forced to do things we are not comfortable doing. That is, when we are pushed out of our comfort zones, our stomachs always keep score. And when we are forced to stay out of our comfort zone, that is, when we are forced to do the things we are not naturals at doing, the greater our chances are of filling one of those 85 per cent of hospital beds.

HORSES FOR COURSES We are always good at the things we feel comfortable doing. We are all 'naturals' at something.

It certainly is 'horses for courses' and 'different strokes for different folks' when it comes to the jobs we do. We all have our part to play. It is when we are miscast for that part, when we become square pegs in round holes, that we become prime candidates for the ulcer and heart-attack wards.

SQUARE PEGS IN ROUND HOLES

THE UNCOMFORTABLE DOVE A Dove has had a proven track record in a job. Everything the Dove has been asked to do has been done willingly and pleasantly with a minimum of fuss. Nothing has been too much trouble. It has been done exactly how it was asked to be done, each time, every time. That is the way Doves are. They are supportive and willing team workers.

Because of this exemplary track record, the Dove is promoted to the position of supervisor. A reward for diligent service.

But this supervisor, because of the nature of the work and the people doing it, is required to be controlling, directive and a disciplinarian, qualities that are unnatural and alien to the Dove.

The doctor and the chemist can look forward to some increased business from this Dove!

THE UNCOMFORTABLE OWL An Owl, who is by natural inclination conservative, methodical, analytical and retiring, is forced by circumstances to adopt a promoting and entrepreneurial role. This requires making contact with strangers and selling the company's products and services. These skills that are not only foreign to the Owl, but are also seen by them as unsavoury to say the least.

There is going to be a run on nerve-rash ointment and antacid pills for this Owl!

THE UNCOMFORTABLE PEACOCK A Peacock, who is a natural extrovert and yearns for interaction with other people, is forced by circumstances into a job that requires hours of solitary, detailed and analytical paper-work, with no contact with the outside world, or chance to talk to other people.

After-hours, these Peacocks are soon going to find themselves with a drink in their hand more often than they used to!

THE UNCOMFORTABLE EAGLE An Eagle, who likes to take charge, be the boss and is a natural doer and result-getter, is forced to become a compliant and supportive follower, with no say in the way things should be done, and no chance of promotion.

Be prepared for lots of disruption to the team from this frustrated Eagle.

PEOPLE AND JOBS

Until we make jobs fit people, rather than people fit jobs, it is arguable that anybody could be totally compatible with any particular job.

Nevertheless, my experience tells me that given a little more thought and effort, we could achieve far better 'fits' whereby people with natural skills and inclinations are doing jobs which call for those natural skills and qualities.

As a result, these people would be far more comfortable, happier and more productive in their jobs.

JOB COMPATABILITY IS THE KEY Please use the learnings from this book and your understanding of yourself to ensure you find the right job for you.

You should have more of an idea of your personality after reading this book. Add this to your natural skills.

Use this knowledge to assist in choosing your career.

We have a JobFit Profiling Tool, available at www.tick.com.au that goes into this in more detail and will give you a full personalised report. Try it – you will find it useful!

"Anyway"

**People are unreasonable, illogical
and self-centred. Love them anyway.**

**If you do good, people will accuse you
of selfish ulterior motives. Do good anyway.**

**If you are successful you win false friends
and true enemies. Succeed anyway.**

**The good you do today will be forgotten
tomorrow. Do good anyway.**

**Honesty and frankness make you vulnerable.
Be honest and frank anyway.**

**People favour underdogs but follow only top
dogs. Fight for some underdogs anyway.**

**What you spend years building may be
destroyed overnight. Build anyway.**

**People really need help but may attack you
if you help them. Help people anyway.**

**Give the world the best you have
and you'll get kicked in the teeth.**

Give the world the best you've got anyway

Author unknown